THOMAS AQUINAS

THOMAS AQUINAS

His Personality and Thought

By

DR. MARTIN GRABMANN

AUTHORIZED TRANSLATION

By VIRGIL MICHEL, O.S.B., PH.D.

NEW YORK
RUSSELL & RUSSELL · INC

1963

𝔑𝔦𝔥𝔦𝔩 𝔒𝔟𝔰𝔱𝔞𝔱: Arthur J. Scanlan, S.T.D., *Censor Librorum*

𝔍𝔪𝔭𝔯𝔦𝔪𝔞𝔱𝔲𝔯: ✠ Patrick Cardinal Hayes, *Archbishop, New York*

New York, July 31, 1928

FIRST PUBLISHED IN 1928
REISSUED, 1963, BY RUSSELL & RUSSELL, INC.
L. C. CATALOG CARD NO: 63—15160

TRANSLATOR'S PREFACE

HE translation of this book was undertaken as a labor of love. As the work progressed, the love never diminished though the labor increased beyond all expectation. That the translation was undertaken at all was due to the belief that a small introductory volume, written by the foremost Thomistic student and research scholar of modern times, should be a welcome addition to the growing body of English literature on what has been called the Scholastic Revival of our day.

In verifying the numerous texts quoted from the works of St. Thomas, it was necessary to compare the German translation with the original Latin and with available English translations. It has been the translator's endeavor to give an English version that most faithfully renders the thought of Thomas. Whether the result is a more intelligible expression of that thought, others must judge. While the non-

[v]

Scholastic mind is probably not set for the task of translating any part of St. Thomas, the modern Scholastic is very prone to read into his words variations of meaning that have developed in Scholastic tradition only after the thirteenth century. Where on a few occasions the German texts of Dr. Grabmann contained elucidating terms or phrases, rendering the thought of St. Thomas more clear to the modern mind, the translator followed suit, since there is probably no living scholar better versed in the study of St. Thomas and of Scholastic sources than Dr. Grabmann.

It is scarcely necessary to state that the present pages constitute a mere introduction to the philosophy of St. Thomas. They are consequently quite inadequate for a full appraisal of the true value of his thought. Still, many may find neither time nor leisure to go beyond such an introductory work. Is it presumptuous to remind them that in judging the thought of another there is no acceptable criterion that does not try to be wholly objective? It is the simplest things that are most true and at times most in need of emphasis. Hence it may be pardonable to suggest to non-Thomistic readers that inability to accept one or both premises of an argument is not of itself an unfailing indication that the statement given as conclusion is false; and to remind readers sympathetic to St. Thomas that belief in a conclusion is of itself no guarantee that the premises or the reasoning are therefore beyond all cavil.

While the work of translation was going on, the original appeared in its fifth revised edition. The many small changes and additions, necessitated by the historical research carried on so vigorously today especially in Scholastic sources, have been embodied in the present volume.

An acknowledgment of thanks to the Reverend Dr. Gerald B. Phelan of St. Michael's College, University of Toronto, scarcely suffices to indicate either the patient care with which he read the translated manuscript or the numerous corrections resulting therefrom. Many improvements in language and in more accurate rendition are due to his valuable suggestions.

V. M.

CONTENTS

THOMAS AQUINAS

THOMAS AQUINAS

PART ONE
Personality of St. Thomas

CHAPTER I

LIFE OF ST. THOMAS

HE figure of the great thinker, Thomas Aquinas, peers out from a comparatively modest framework of life. Rocca Sicca, the hereditary castle of the counts of Aquino in the Neapolitan province, can boast of having given to the world the greatest theologian of the Middle Ages. Thomas was born there at the end of 1224 or the beginning of 1225, the son of Count Landulph of Aquin and of Theodora, born countess of Theate. At the age of five Thomas was brought to the monastery of Monte Cassino, nearby, where he received his education under the watchful eye of his uncle, the Abbot Sinibald. The sacred solitude of

[1]

the holy mountain of Cassino may have permanently influenced the susceptible heart of the ideally-minded boy, and have developed in him his bent for reflection, contemplation, and the inner life. Thomas left Monte Cassino in 1239 in order to pursue the study of the liberal arts in Naples. His teacher in the trivium (grammar, rhetoric, dialectic) was Master Martin. His teacher in the subjects of the quadrivium (arithmetic, geometry, astronomy, and music) was Peter of Ireland (Petrus Hibernus). Being the author of unpublished commentaries on Aristotle, he probably gave the youthful Thomas his first acquaintance with writings of Aristotle. With his increase of knowledge the young nobleman grew also in piety and zeal for virtue. No wonder that the white garb of the new Order of Preachers attracted him strongly. In 1244 the son of the count of Aquin received the habit of St. Dominic in S. Domenico Maggiore, Naples, at the hands of the Prior, Thomas Agni. In the same year his religious superiors sent him to Paris for higher studies. But his brothers, Rainald and Landulph, incensed at his entry into the order, forcibly interrupted his journey and held him captive for a year in the paternal castle of S. Giovanni. After again attaining his freedom, Thomas was accompanied to Paris by no less a person than John the Teuton of Wildhausen, General of the Order.

It was in 1245 that Thomas for the first time set

foot in the capital of France, called "the city of philosophers" by Albert the Great and praised by Armand of Bellovisu as "the greatest centre of theological knowledge." Surely he did not suspect at the time that he would become the most famous professor of the University. It was now the first meeting took place between Thomas, the young Sicilian Dominican, and Albert the German, surnamed the Great, who by this time was a highly esteemed theologian of the order. For three years, 1245–1248, Thomas sat at the feet of Albert in Paris. When the general chapter of the order, held at Paris in 1248, charged Albert with the task of instituting a general house of studies in Cologne for the German province of the Dominicans, Thomas followed his beloved teacher to that city and there spent four years of serious study. Albert the Great exerted a powerful influence on the intellectual development of Aquinas. A copy of Albert's lectures on Pseudo-Dionysius from the pen of Thomas is preserved in Naples. A Vatican text (Cod. Vat. lat. 722) and other manuscripts discovered by A. Pelzer contain: "*Questiones fratris Alberti ordinis predicatorum quas collegit magister frater Thomas de Aquino:* Questions of Brother Albert of the order of preachers, collected by Master Brother Thomas of Aquin." They are unpublished lectures of Albert on the Nichomachean Ethics edited by Thomas.

[3]

In 1252 Thomas was again in Paris, where he began his teaching career as a bachelor by lecturing on
Peter the Lombard's *Books of Sentences*. It was just
at the outbreak of the bitter conflict between the professors of the University belonging to the secular
clergy (headed by William of St. Amour) and their
colleagues of the Dominican and Franciscan orders,
who excelled them in scholarly attainments. Thomas
entered into the fray and defended the rights of his
order in a treatise "*Contra impugnantes Dei cultum
et religionem:* Against those who attack the worship
of God and the religious life." Because of the general disorders, which were only ended by the inter-
position of Pope Alexander VI in favor of the orders, Thomas was not officially received into the ranks
of the masters at the time set down in the statutes
of the University. The same is true of Bonaventure,
the Franciscan theologian, who defended the rights
of the Friars Minor.

In 1256 Thomas, together with Bonaventure, ob-
tained his licentiate, the *licentia docendi*,[1] from the
Chancellor Heimericus. He could now deliver his
inaugural lecture (*principium*), and teach on his own

[1] The chancellor of the Church of Notre Dame in Paris in the
name of the Pope gave the licentiate to the bachelor presented to him,
who had fulfilled the proper requirements. The licentiate was a
permission for the independent exercise of the academic power of
teaching. The candidate thus promoted was now admitted into the
ranks of the college of professors, and began his public teaching
career as *Master* with an inaugural lecture, called the *principium*.

[4]

responsibility as master of theology, as ordinary professor. Nevertheless the opposing teachers for some time continued their refusal to receive him formally into the college of professors.

Thomas' task as teacher was now the explanation of the Sacred Scriptures, which formed the regular textbook of theological instruction. He looked upon his duty as professor of theology with a serious mind. He had a high conception of the position of the teacher of theology. In a passage of his (*Quodl.* l. 14), he touches upon the question, whether the pastors of souls or the professors of theology have a more important position in the life of the Church, and he decides in favor of the latter. He gives the following reason for his view: In the construction of a building the architect, who conceives the plan and directs the construction, stands above the workmen who actually put up the building. In the construction of the divine edifice of the Church and the care of souls, the position of architect is held by the bishops, but also by the theology professors, who study and teach the manner in which the care of souls is to be conducted. How seriously Thomas looked upon his work can also be seen from various utterances in the occasional writings which, in his ever-ready spirit of service, he composed at the request of persons seeking his advice. In the work he addressed to the Duchess of Brabant " On the Treatment of Jews "

[5]

he speaks of the "many labors connected with the profession of teaching." In the treatise *De sortibus* (On Lots) he states that he is using the time of vacation in order to give a desired solution. This serious and exclusive devotion to his profession, a devotion exercised with the full energy of a richly endowed mind rendered ever more fruitful and intense by means of a tireless literary activity, brought Thomas into high repute at the University. As his competent biographer, William of Tocco, relates, he was praised especially for the originality, the progressiveness, and the independence of his lectures: "He brought new articles into his lectures, instituted a new and clear method of scientific investigation and synthesis, and developed new proofs in his argumentation. Every one who thus heard him teach new things and solve doubts and difficulties with new arguments, could not but believe that God had illumined this thinker with rays of a new light." Thomas was not a professor who could perform his task by walking in old paths and satisfying himself with old ideas. Up to the present there has been some question about the number of pupils that Thomas attracted to himself. We shall show in another place that his high gift of teaching and his devotion to his calling resulted in a large number of faithful and inspired disciples, a fact hitherto not sufficiently appreciated. Thomas taught in Paris till 1259, during part of that time together with his fellow Dominican, Peter of Tarantasia, later Pope Innocent V.

In 1259 Thomas attended the general chapter of his order at Valenciennes, where his teaching experience was well employed in helping to organize the curriculum of studies for the Dominican schools. He worked out the ideas of this curriculum in conjunction with the masters Bonushomo, Florentius, Albert the Great, and Peter of Tarantasia, leaving room in the curriculum for the proper treatment of profane studies. At this same chapter it was decided to erect schools for the Dominican missions in Spain. In connection with this decision and at the instigation of Raymond of Penafort, Thomas wrote his *Summa contra gentes* in Italy from about 1259–1264. This work was to be the teaching and study manual of the Dominican missionaries of Spain.

For the greater part of the decade 1260–70 Thomas taught theology in his native Italy, from which he had been absent fifteen years. From 1261–64 he was at the papal court of Urban IV. The cities in which this court was held, Orvieto and Viterbo, have retained memories of his stay down to our own day. Some of his works (*Catena aurea, Contra errores Græcorum*) were composed for Urban IV or dedicated to him. During this time he also took part in the institution of the feast of Corpus Christi by composing the office of the feast, and the wonderful eucharistic hymns. It was also at the court of Urban that Thomas learned to know his confrere, the linguist William of Moerbeke, and induced him to translate works of Aristotle into Latin directly from the Greek. In this way his commentaries on Aristotle, dating mainly from this Italian sojourn, as well as his later studies of Aristotle, attained a degree of philological reliability and accuracy that could not be found in the Aristotelian translations from the Arabian of Gerard of Cremona, Michael Scot, etc. The following remark, from the curial poem of the master, Henry the Poet, of Wuerzburg, edited by Grauert, seems to apply to the sojourn of St. Thomas at the court of Urban IV: " There (at the house of the Pope) is one who would become the founder of a new philosophy, if the old philosophy were lying in ruins. As a new editor he would rebuild it in a better fashion; he would excel the old philosophers by the fame of his learning."

Clement IV, the successor of Urban, also esteemed the talent and virtue of Thomas, and offered him the archiepiscopal chair of Naples. By dint of prayers and tears the humility of Thomas conquered, and he was allowed to retain the position of a simple religious and to devote himself exclusively to the profession of learning. In 1265 the provincial chapter of the Dominicans at Anagni called him to Rome to supervise the studies of the order for the Roman province. He taught with his customary zeal in the quiet convent of Santa Sabina on the Aventine, where Dominic himself had labored. From 1267 on, Thomas was presumably again active as lector at Viterbo, at the court of Clement IV. His labors in Italy left him more leisure than his teaching in Paris had given him, and he used it for the composition of numerous literary works, especially for the commencement of his most mature work, the *Summa theologica,* the first part of which was written at S. Sabina in Rome.

A larger field of labor was assigned to him in the fall of 1268, when his superiors recalled him to the University of Paris as professor of theology. This second sojourn in Paris 1268–1272 marks the highest scientific achievement in the career of Thomas. It is a period of most fruitful literary labor for him, as well as one of severe conflicts.

The aversion of the professors of the secular clergy at Paris for the two mendicant orders, smouldering since 1256, was again in high flame. The attacks on the Franciscan and Dominican professors were led by Gerard of Abbeville, a very able man, whose *Quæstiones quodlibetales* give good testimony of his learning, and by Nicholas of Lisieux. By the force of his high scholarly repute and by means of two counter attacks (*Contra doctrinam retrahentium a*

religione; De perfectione vitæ spiritualis) Thomas
stood out against these enemies as an impenetrable
wall.

Much more important was another battle that
Thomas had to fight out in Paris. It was his victori-
ous struggle as leader of a Christian Peripateticism
against the Averroistic Peripateticism of the Paris
university. Under the leadership of Siger of Brabant
and Boethius of Dacia, Averroism had arisen within
the ranks of the faculty of arts as a powerful cur-
rent of thought. For the Averroists, Averroes' interpretation of Aristotelean thought was normative.
They made their very own even those teachings of
the Arabian philosopher which ran counter to theological doctrine. Among such teachings were the
doctrine of the eternity of the world, the denial of
providence, the denial of free will and, especially,
the doctrine of the numerical unity of the intellectual
soul in all men. The study of philosophy was esteemed as the highest value in human life, in total
disregard of faith and revelation. The picture of
this gigantic intellectual movement, portrayed by
P. Mandonnet in his monumental work, is now better
understood in the light of the unpublished and hitherto unknown Questions of Siger of Brabant, which
I discovered in the Munich library (Clm. 9559).
Over against this Averroistic Aristotelianism Thomas
set up a Christian Aristotelianism; that is, an Aris-

totelian philosophy judged, purged, and corrected on the basis of the teaching of the Church. In a special tract, " *De unitate intellectus contra Averroistas:* On the Unity of the Intellect against the Averroists " (or, according to a Munich manuscript, Clm. 8001 fol. 29r: " Tract of Brother Thomas against Master Siger on the Unity of the Intellect "), he most decidedly rejects monopsychism, the momentous error of Siger, and shows that on this point Aristotle had been misinterpreted. The matter was a theological question of the greatest importance at the time, as can be gathered from the emotion apparent in the closing words of Thomas, who is otherwise so calm and mild-tempered: " This is our refutation of the error. It is not based on the documents of faith, but on the reasons and the pronouncements of the philosophers themselves. If anyone, who boastfully prides himself on his supposed wisdom, desires to say anything against our exposition, let him not do it in some corner nor before boys who are entirely without judgment in such difficult matters. Let him rather write against this our tract, if he has the requisite courage. He will then find not only myself, the least of them all, but many others, cultivators of truth, who will step up against his error, and attack his lack of knowledge." Thomas witnessed the condemnation of Averroism by the Bishop of Paris on December 10, 1270. Siger of Brabant, in fact, did not hold undisputed sway in the faculty of arts. Thomas himself had many devoted disciples among its members. Thus Peter of Auvergne, a professor of that faculty, is designated as " the most faithful disciple " of Thomas. It was he who completed Thomas' commentaries on Aristotle's " Concerning Heaven and the World " and his " Politics." The scientific refutation of Averroistic Aristotelianism was celebrated in the art of the Middle Ages as one of Thomas' outstanding achievements. A large fresco by Andrea de Bonaiuto in the Spanish chapel at Florence, altar pictures by Filippino Lippi in the Church of S. Maria sopra Minerva in Rome, and by Fr. Traini in the church of St. Catherine in Pisa, and a tempera painting by Benozzo Gozzoli in the Louvre, significantly represent " the Triumph of St. Thomas " over Averroes, the latter sprawling at the feet of the former.

For Thomas there was still a third battle to fight in Paris, one that was probably the most distasteful to his noble mind, the scientific altercation with the Franciscan theologians. The condemnation of the Averroistic Peripateticism also cast a shadow on the Christian Aristotelianism championed by Albert the Great and Thomas. For a long time the latter had been viewed askance by rigorously conservative theologians of the secular clergy, and particularly of the Franciscan order. Even some fellow-Dominicans, especially among the English (Robert Kilwardby),

opposed the new scientific tendency taken up by
Thomas. For all of these theologians, St. Augustine
was the master thinker, not only in theological but
also in philosophical questions; and they used the
ideas and texts of Aristotle rather as ornaments and
methodological aids. Thomas, too, considered Augustine beyond all doubt the greatest of the Church
Fathers, and the most esteemed authority in theology.
But he also gave Aristotle an important position.
Aristotle furnished him with ideas and points of
view that aided in developing and constructing theological speculation; and in philosophy, especially in
psychology and epistemology, he was the master
mind. The Augustinian tradition was to be reconciled
with his thought by a concordistic interpretation wherever possible or necessary. Hence a heated dispute
arose between the conservative Augustinianism of the
above-mentioned theologians and the progressive
Aristotelianism of Albert the Great and Thomas.
The Franciscan theologian, John Peckam, chief of
the opponents of Thomas, attacked the latter vigorously. The principal point of contention was the
Thomistic doctrine of the unity of the substantial
form in man. Throughout this time, as John Peckham subsequently (in letters dating from 1284 and
1285) stated with admiration, Thomas explained his
views and his orthodoxy to his colleagues with the
greatest calmness and humility, and finally submitted

[13]

the entire matter to the judgment of the college of theological professors at Paris.

The various controversies and disturbances in no way deprived Thomas of his holy peace of soul and his love for literary labor. An end was however put to all these activities by his religious superiors who called him away from Paris after Easter of the year 1272. His successor was Fr. Romanus, O.Pr., whose unprinted commentary on the *Sentences* is more Augustinian in tendency. The recall of Thomas caused the greatest surprise among the Paris professors, and found no favor with them, as we can see from the petitions they vainly addressed to the general chapter of the Dominicans meeting in Florence June 1272, to have Thomas sent back to his chair at Paris.

Thomas again set foot on his native soil. The Dominican chapter of the Roman province of the order, which had also met at Florence in 1272, charged him with the erection and organization of its general theological curriculum. Thomas was free to choose his own location and was given the widest powers in the exercise of his task. He decided on Naples, partly, at least at the instance of the king, Charles of Anjou. Here the youthful Thomas had made his first studies, here his soul had sought God in the peace of the conventual life of St. Dominic; and it was Naples that now attracted him at the height of his mature age, of his ascetic life, of his intellectual labors. Did he have any inkling that only a few years of life were left him?

In 1274 Thomas was again called away from his quiet labors in Naples. Pope Gregory X summoned him to attend the Council of Lyons, which was to treat the question of Church union. In this question the Pope did not want to be without the expert counsel of the famous theologian. Thomas had proved himself a thorough student of the problem both in his larger works as also in monographs (*Contra errores Græcorum:* Against the Errors of the Greeks).

The road to the council was for Thomas the road to death. The source accounts of the last years of Thomas indicate clearly that he was exhausted and overworked, that his bodily vigor had not been able to keep pace with his astounding mental energy. The hand of death stretched out for him before he could reach Rome. He stopped for rest in the Cistercian monastery of Fossanuova, near Terracina, and there he died the death of a saint, March 7, 1274. At the reception of the Eucharist on his death-bed, he made this statement: " I receive Thee, redeeming Price of my soul. Out of love for Thee have I studied, watched through many nights, and exerted myself; Thee did I preach and teach. I have never said aught against Thee. Nor do I persist stubbornly in my views. If I have ever expressed myself er-

roneously on this Sacrament, I submit to the judgment of the holy Roman Church, in the obedience
of which I now part from this world." Reginald of
Piperno, the inseparable friend and companion of
Thomas, than whom none had a deeper insight into
his pure, childlike soul, and who heard the confession
of his dying teacher and friend, later on testified
that he had found Thomas as pure and innocent as a
child of five years. The monks of Fossanuova, to
whom Thomas explained the Canticle of Canticles on
his death-bed, were under the impression of having
witnessed the departure of a saint. A beautiful relief
by Bernini, now gracing the death-chamber of
Thomas, represents the latter in the act of explaining this canticle of love to the reverently absorbed
monks.

The news of his death aroused deep sorrow in dis-
tant Paris. The University mourned the premature
death of a genial, assiduous, and noble scholar, who
had been their honor and their pride. The Paris
faculty of arts, writing to the general chapter of the
Dominicans, held in Florence 1274, dedicated a
touching *In Memoriam* to their departed colleague.
In terms almost extravagant they commemorate
Thomas as the beacon, the sun of the century, and
they deeply deplore that his death has deprived the
Church of the rays of such a brilliant light. To these
laudatory words is added the petition, that the re-

mains of Thomas be given a final resting place in
Paris; for it is entirely unfitting and unbecoming
that any other city should bury and preserve his remains than that Paris which reared him, nourished
and cultivated him, and which later received such
inexpressible advancement through him. His memory, which would indeed endure forever by reason of
his writings at the Paris university, should then be
implanted more firmly in the hearts of following
generations by a worthy monument to him.

This request of the faculty of arts was not granted.
The remains of Thomas were after various vicissi-
tudes finally interred in the Dominican church of
Toulouse, 1368. Since the French revolution they
lie in the church of St. Sernin of the same city.

CHAPTER II

LITERARY LABORS OF ST. THOMAS

HE literary labors of St. Thomas are astonishing in their extent; the more so, since he never reached the age of fifty, and since much of his time was taken up by teaching and by the various practices of his religious life. As often happens with Scholastic writers, some apocryphal works have been included in the traditional list of the writings of Thomas. But much work has been done in the critical investigation of the texts and writings, notably by Barbavara, Anthony of Sena, Nicolai, J. Echard, de Rubeis, and in more recent times by P. A. Uccelli, H. Denifle, and P. Mandonnet. The task of sifting the genuine from the spurious works is made possible through the preservation of old and reliable catalogues of the writings of St. Thomas, and the examination of the tradition handed down in manuscripts.

Accordingly it is possible to put together the following list of works as certainly genuine. Since a judgment on the views of Thomas must be greatly guided by the dates of composition, the latter will be indicated as far as possible.

A. PHILOSOPHICAL WRITINGS

    I. Commentaries on Aristotle:

        1. On *Perihermeneias* (1269–1271?).
        2. On the second two *Analytics*.
        3. On the ten books of *Ethics* (1261–1264).
        4. On the twelve books of *Metaphysics* (1271–1272).
        5. On the eight books of *Physics* (1261–1264).
        6. On the three books *On the Soul* (1270–1272).
        7. On the treatise *On Sense Perception* (*De sensu et sensato*).
        8. On the book *On Memory and Reminiscence*.
        9. On the first three books of the treatise *On Heaven and Earth* up to L. III. lect. 8 (1272).
      10. On the books *On Generation and Corruption of the things of nature* L. I. lect. 1–17 (1272).
      11. On the *Politics* (Books 1–3, 6) (1272).
      12. On the books *On Meteorology* up to L. II. lect. 10 (1269–1271?).

II. Commentary on the *Liber de causis* (after 1268).

III. Smaller philosophical writings (*Opuscula*):

1. *De occultis operationibus naturæ* (On the hidden activities of nature).

2. *De principiis naturæ* (On the principles of nature).

3. *De mixtione elementorum* (On the mixture of the elements).

4. *De motu cordis* (On the motion of the heart).

5. *De ente et essentia* (On existence and essence).

6. *De æternitate mundi contra mumurantes* (On the eternity of the world, written about 1270).

7. *De unitate intellectus contra Averroistas* (Polemic on the unity of the intellect against the commentary on *De anima* by Siger of Brabant. 1270).

8. *De substantiis separatis* (On the spiritual substances existing independently of matter. After 1268).

9. *De quattuor oppositis* (On the fourfold opposition of propositions).

10. *De propositionibus modalibus* (On modal propositions).

11. *De demonstratione* (On scientific demonstration).

12. *De fallaciis* (On fallacies).

13. *De natura accidentis* (On the nature of accident).

14. *De natura generis* (On the notion of genus).

15. *De natura verbi intellectus* (On the nature of the mental word).

16. *De differentia verbi divini et humani* (On the difference between the divine and the human word).

17. *De natura materiæ* (On the nature of matter).

18. *De instantibus* (On the instantaneous).

19. *De principio individuationis* (On the principle of individuation).

20. *De fato* (On fate — perhaps by Albert the Great).

B. WORKS CHIEFLY THEOLOGICAL IN CONTENT
    I. General expositions of systematic theology:
        1. Commentary on the *Four Books of Sentences* of Peter the Lombard (1253–1255). A later commentary of Thomas on the first book of the *Sentences* has been lost.
        2. *Compendium theologiæ ad Reginaldum*

(brief, incomplete outline of theology, written after 1260).

3. *Summa theologica.* The first (Prima) and the second (Secunda) parts of the theological *summa* date from the years 1266–1272. The third part (Tertia), written 1272–1273, remained unfinished. Its completion (the so-called *Supplementum*) is from the hand of Reginald of Piperno.

II. The *Quæstiones:*

 1. *Quæstiones quodlibetales* [2] (Books 1–6 written in Paris, 1269–1272; Books 7–11, in Italy, 1265–1267).

 2. *Quæstiones disputatæ.* [3]

   (a) *De veritate* (On truth, 1256–1259).

   (b) *De potentia* (On the power of God, 1260–1268).

[2] The *Quæstiones quodlibetales* are the literary résumés of the free disputations held twice a year, before Christmas and Easter, and were made by the master of theology who instituted them and presided at them. In these disputations questions from the entire field of philosophy were discussed. Hence there is no systematic arrangement of matter in the scholastic literature of the *Quodlibeta.*

[3] The *Quæstiones disputatæ* are the literary résumés of the ordinary disputations conducted at regular intervals by a theology professor. In them important theological problems were treated more thoroughly and profoundly than usual. The *Quæstiones disputatæ* of Thomas, as of other scholastics, e.g., of Matthew of Aquasparta, are therefore more complete, coherent, and profound expositions of theological questions. Later on the distinction between the *Quæstiones quodlibetales* and the *Quæstiones disputatæ* was lost.

(c) *De spiritualibus creaturis* (On the spiritual creatures, 1260–1268).

(d) *De anima* (On the soul, 1260–1268).

(e) *De unione Verbi incarnati* (On the Incarnation of Christ, 1260–1268).

(f) *De malo* (On evil, 1260–1268).

(g) *De virtutibus in communi* (On the virtues in general, 1269–1272).

(h) *De virtutibus cardinalibus* (On the cardinal virtues, 1269–1272).

(i) *De caritate* (On charity, 1269–1272).

(k) *De correctione fraterna* (On fraternal correction, 1269–1272).

(l) *De spe* (On hope 1269–1272).

(m) *De beatitudine* (On happiness, 1269–1272).

III. Smaller works (*Opuscula*), chiefly on points of dogma:

1. *De articulis fidei et sacramentis* (On the articles of faith and the sacraments).

[23]

2. *In Dionysium de divinis nominibus* (Exposition of the work of Dionysius the Areopagite on the names of God).

3. *In Boethium de trinitate* (Exposition of the treatise of Boethius on the Trinity).

4. *In Boethium de hebdomadibus* (Exposition of the treatise of Boethius on the axioms).

5. *In primum decretalem* (Explanation of the first decretal).

6. *In secundum decretalem* (Explanation of the second decretal).

7. *Responsio de articulis XXXVI* (Answers to questions directed to Thomas).

8. *Responsio de articulis XLII* (Idem, 1271).

9. *Responsio de articulis CVIII* (Idem).

10. *Articuli iterum remissi* (Idem).

11. *Responsio de articulis VI* (Idem).

12. *Responsio ad Bernardum abbatem* (Letter to Abbot Bernard Ayglerius of Monte Cassino).

IV. Apologetic works:

1. *Summa contra gentes* (Summa against the heathens, i.e., chiefly against the Arabians, 1259–1264. Autograph preserved in the Vatican library).

2. *De rationibus fidei contra Saracenos, Græcos et Armenos* (The foundations of faith established against the Saracens, Greeks, and Armenians).

3. *Contra errores Græcorum* (Against the errors of the Greeks, 1261–1264).

V. Practical theology, philosophy of right, social right, the state:

1. *De sortibus* (On casting lots).

2. *De judiciis astrorum* (On astrology. After 1260).

3. *De forma absolutionis* (On the formula of absolution).

4. *De emptione et venditione* (On buying and selling).

5. *De regimine principum ad regem Cypri* (On the rule of princes. Books I and II, c. 1–4, are by Thomas, probably about 1266; the rest is by Ptolomy of Lucca).

6. *De regimine Judæorum ad ducissam Brabantiæ* (On the treatment of Jews by civic rulers, 1263–1267?).

VI. Asceticism and religious life:

1. *Expositio Orationis dominicæ* (Explanation of the Our Father).

2. *Expositio Symboli Apostolorum* (Analysis of the Apostles' Creed).

3. *De duobus præceptis caritatis et decem legis præceptis* (On the Commandments of Love, and the Decalogue).

4. *Officium Corporis Christi* (The office of Corpus Christi, with the eucharistic hymns, 1264).

5. *Collationes dominicales* (Sunday sermons).

6. *Epistola ad quendam fratrem de modo studendi* (Letter to a religious confrere on a fruitful method of study).

7. *Contra impugnantes Dei cultum et religionem* (In defense of the religious state, 1256 or 1257).

8. *De perfectione vitæ spiritualis* (Idem, 1269).

9. *Contra retrahentes a religioso cultu* (Idem, 1270).

10. *Expositio de Ave Maria* (Explanation of the Hail Mary).

11. Two newly discovered *Principia* (Inaugural addresses, as bachelor 1252, and as master 1256).

VII. Exegetical writings:

1. On the Book of Job.

2. On the first four nocturns of the Psalter (to Ps. 54).

3. On the Canticle of Canticles (lost).

4. On Isaias.
5. On Jeremias.
6. On the Lamentations.
7. *Catena aurea super IV Evangelia* (Golden chain. An explanation of the four Gospels by linking together quotations from the Fathers. The catena of Matthew was written between 1261 and 1264; the others were completed before 1272).
8. Lectures on the Gospel of Matthew, held in Paris.
9. Lectures on the Gospel of John (put together by Reginald of Piperno, 1269–1272).
10. Explanations of the Letters of St. Paul (Commentary on the Letter to the Romans, and on I. Cor. 1–10 by Thomas himself; the rest is a faithful transcription of his lectures by Reginald of Piperno. Approximately from 1269–1273).

CHAPTER III

ST. THOMAS AS SCHOLAR

N HIS contemporaries Thomas made the impression of a most gifted scholar and powerful personality. Bartholomew of Lucca calls him the " ark of philosophy and theology "; John of Colonna, the " incomparable teacher "; Fra Remigio de Girolami calls him " The light of our eyes, the crown of our heads." Other members of his order, Bernard of Clermont, Armandus of Bellovisu, and especially William of Tocco, speak of his eminent personality in terms of enthusiasm bordering on the extreme. Nor was this impression confined to the men of his own order. Even Siger of Brabant speaks of " the outstanding men in philosophy, Albert and Thomas." The secular priest, Godfrey of Fontaines, professor at Paris, differed from Thomas on many points. But he is full of the highest praise for this " most famous teacher," and says that the teaching of Thomas is

the most useful and praiseworthy after that of the Fathers, and that the teachings of other theologians attain their correct perspective, their agreeableness, and their spice only through him.

It is therefore no easy task to attempt an analysis of the personality of Thomas, and especially of his individual character as a scholar. There is, above all, no extant correspondence, such as gives us the surprising glimpses into the soul of Anselm of Canterbury. Then his biographer, William of Tocco, is by no means so fine a depicter of the soul as is Eadmer, the biographer of Anselm. Furthermore Thomas had little occasion for writings of a more practical nature, which would inevitably have more personal color in them, such as St. Bonaventure had to write extensively as General of the Franciscans. The works of Thomas furnish the chief basis for a delineation of his erudite personality; and they were written in such a rigorously matter-of-fact and impersonal manner that only an extended and profound study of them will reveal something of the personal character of their author. In any study of the scientific mentality of Thomas, account must also be taken of the spiritual traits of his soul everywhere in evidence.

Like Augustine, Anselm of Canterbury, and Hugo of St. Victor before him, Thomas called attention to the importance of an ethical and religious disposition of soul for the deeper study of supersensory and supernatural truths. Even Plato had recognized and asserted that the full knowledge of the true and the eternal is possible only to the soul that is free from the sensuous. What Thomas taught concerning the relation of moral purity, love of God, and the gifts of the Holy Ghost to theological speculation, he also lived in his own person. The picture of Thomas the scholar cannot be separated from his ethical and religious personality. The student in Thomas cannot be understood without Thomas the saint.

With unmistakable love did Fra Angelico, confrere of Thomas, and of kindred soul, paint the person of Thomas. For him Thomas is ever the profound thinker, standing above the affairs of earthly life, occupied with the sublimest mysteries; not a cold and rigid intellectual figure, but an attractive personality, breathing a charming amiability. The same portrait peers out of the biographies of William of Tocco, Bernard Guido, and Peter Calo. The testimonies of the witnesses at the canonization, based chiefly on Reginald of Piperno and John of Caitia, two disciples and friends of Thomas, agree almost to a word in presenting a number of traits that readily combine into a truthful and impressive characterization.

According to these testimonies Thomas was entirely free from worldly inclinations and ambitions, a picture of stainless innocence and purity and of ideal devotion of heart and mind to God. Only a short time was set aside by him for eating and sleep. He read Mass at a very early hour and thereupon assisted at another. If he did not himself celebrate, he attended two Masses. His whole day was occupied with prayer, teaching, and writing. He never took up his pen without a preliminary prayer to God, often in tears. In order to employ his time to the utmost, he would dictate to several scribes at once. He was ever collected and contemplative. No idle word escaped his lips. So far was he removed from worldly occupation, that even at table the divine occupied his thought, and he was not aware of what went on about him. Thus, William of Tocco tells us, even at the table of Louis the Saint, King of France, Thomas forgot his environment, and suddenly pounded on the table exclaiming: " Now I have a decisive argument against the Manichæans." For this reason his solicitous superiors, as the same biographer reports, appointed Reginald of Piperno as his companion (*socius*), who was to keep a watchful eye on the learned professor ever moving in the upper regions of thought, and to see that he would properly take the required food and, in general, keep his bearings in the contingencies of practical life.

In Thomas the exclusive devotion to a higher world was accompanied by an extraordinary amiability and astounding humility. These qualities captivated all who came in contact with him, and helped to soften much opposition.

In his *Banquet* (*Convivio*) Dante calls Thomas the " good Brother Thomas," and this is in full conformity with the picture of humility and kindness which the oldest biographers and the acts of canonization paint for us. He was never angry because of untoward happenings. In disputations, in which the participants so readily became heated, he was mild and humble and never guilty of an overbearing word. His scholarly opponent, John Peckham, praises this trait. In a letter of 1285 he relates that he had attacked Thomas vigorously, but that the latter had answered " with great mildness and humility." Another indication of this disposition is found in the fact that he earnestly begged of God in prayer ever to remain a simple religious. Many traits and happenings attest to his kindness of heart. In his smaller writings he answers problems directed to him, with the greatest willingness. Often the introductory or the concluding remarks of these treatises show an ideal unselfishness. For his family he always preserved a warm place in his heart, even at the height of his scientific labors and reputation. Another beautiful and Christian trait of his soul was his fidelity in friendship. His friendly relation with Bonaventure, narrated in the oldest sources, has often been praised.

More touching still is his friendship with Reginald of Piperno, his constant companion especially in later years, and the trusted witness of his rich interior life, to whom Thomas dedicated some of his writings. Thus his *Compendium theologiæ* is prefaced by the words: " To Brother Reginald, most dear of companions." It is regretful, indeed, that Reginald followed his teacher, friend, and charge to the grave so soon, and thus lost the opportunity of depicting the life and the soul of Thomas for posterity. Albert the Great, teacher of Thomas, seems to have been very close to him also in his later years. In the acts of canonization it is related that after the death of Thomas, Albert could not hear his name pronounced without bursting into tears, and that in his ripe old age he made the long journey from Cologne to Paris in order to defend the views of his great disciple. In the lives of many thinkers of the Middle Ages we find indications of a nobility of soul that is often sought in vain in the lives of modern savants.

We have now glimpsed Thomas the saint. Let us review the outstanding features of the savant. The fundamental traits of Thomas, devotion to the supersensory and the divine, and his humble peace of soul, also had their influence on his scientific pursuits, on the nature of his scholarly personality.

We shall perhaps get the clearest notion of the scientific mentality of Thomas by examining the goal of his laborious study and the means he used to attain it.

For Thomas the aim of his life of study and intellectual endeavor is the profound penetration into the domain of the supersensory and supernatural truths, the universal eager search for the causes, relations, laws, and forces, of the natural and supernatural world. The entire order of the universe and of its causes should impress itself upon the soul (*De verit.* 2, 2). A knowledge of the highest things, even if imperfect here on earth, gives to the human mind its highest perfection (*Contra gentes* I, 5). Theology, the sacred science, is considered " *quædam impressio divinæ scientiæ* — the stamp of divine knowledge in the human mind " (*S. th.* I, 1, 3 ad 2), a participation in the very knowledge of God and a foretaste of the knowledge of God in heaven, — a conception of the Christian teaching on God that received a majestic expression in the *Disputa* of Raphael.

For the attainment of this high goal of erudition Thomas walks the road of independent speculative reflection, using the materials of previous study and taking into account also the ethico-religious aspects of the problems. Thomas therefore reveals himself as a mind characterized by independent speculation that seeks logical and metaphysical foundations, by a positive historical method of scrutiny and research, and by a deeply religious and mystical bent.

The work of Thomas is above all indepedent in its logical methodology and its metaphysical speculation. His labors were guided by strictly impersonal motives and dominated only by his high ideal of truth. " In accepting or rejecting opinions, a man must not be influenced by love or hatred of him who proffers the opinions but only by the certainty of the truth " (*In XII Metaph.*, lect. 9). Everywhere Thomas walks the narrow path of truth, and to the utmost of his ability seeks light and clarity on the problems before him. He starts out from previous results, utilizes the conclusions already attained, adds proof to proof, observation to observation, until the solution sought stands out clearly. Everywhere he separates real from apparent knowledge, the certain from the probable, definite conclusions from hypotheses. Pierre Duhem, historian of the Copernican cosmic system, considers it the high merit of Thomas to have taken the following stand in regard to the Ptolemaic astronomy (*In II. De cœlo et mundo*, lect. 17; *Summa theologica* I, 32, a. 1 ad 2): The hypotheses on which an astronomical system is based do not become demonstrated truths by the very fact that their deductions agree with observations.[1]

In his search for truth and clarity Thomas never avoided difficulties. It lay in the scholastic method

[1] P. Duhem, *Essai sur la notion de Théorie physique de Platon à Galiléi*, Paris, 1908, p. 46 ff.

of presentation to give all the pros and cons of a problem. Thereupon it stated a definite position of its own, and then refuted the opposing views (Statement: *Videtur quod non*; counter statement: *Sed contra*; main body or *corpus articuli: Respondeo dicendum*; criticism of rejected views: *Ad primum dicendum*, etc.). For Thomas this scheme did not tend towards dialectical artificiality, but was employed in the interests of a practical methodical doubt. The replies to objections often contain remarks that would have disturbed the trend of argument in the body. In many of his works, as in the *Summa contra gentes* and the *Opuscula*, Thomas abandons the scholastic technic entirely and presents his views and arguments with complete freedom of expression.

Thomas strictly avoids exaggerations. Subtle questions, that admit of no true answer, he leaves aside. Printed and unprinted *Sentences* (a type of theological textbook) of the twelfth century contain very many subtleties, which were taken over into the literature of the thirteenth century as a precious heritage, but which are dropped by him. Nor is he a friend of the tendency to exaggerated dogmatism. " Nothing may be asserted as true that is opposed to the truth of faith, to revealed dogma. But it is neither permissible to take whatever we hold to be true, and present it as an article of faith. For the truth of our faith becomes a matter of ridicule among

[36]

the infidels, if any Catholic, not gifted with the necessary scientific learning, presents as a dogma what scientific scrutiny shows to be false " (*De pot.* 4, 1).

In his search for truth Thomas corrected, supplemented, or retracted his own earlier views, whenever new matter or deeper knowledge proved them to be inadequate or erroneous. A comparison of his earliest extensive work, the commentary on the *Books of Sentences,* and his *Summa theologica,* the most mature summary of his theological thought, reveals many such internal steps of progress in his thought. This is also seen in the collections of discrepancies between the above commentary and *summa* that have come down to us from the beginning of the fourteenth century.

In his research Thomas admirably combined observation and speculation, analysis and synthesis. He strikes a middle course between a one-sided emphasis on the factual at the expense of ideal truth, and a one-sided emphasis of the ideal at the expense of the factual — between a positivistic empiricism and an exaggerated idealism. His view on the nature of feeling is characterized by a considerable measure of psychological observation. It is precisely the facts of experience that cause him to adhere closely to the Aristotelian theory of knowledge, and to recede from the Augustinian views championed by the Franciscan school. In observation and knowledge of the natural sciences, he is inferior to Albert the Great and Roger Bacon. But in his ethical, social, and political studies he brings in a noteworthy collection of observed data. Simon Deploige has shown in detail how Thomas displayed a true sense for the reality of things and made surprisingly rich observations in ethical and sociological questions.[2] Thomas does not stop at observation. He always endeavors to attain the real nature, causes, laws, and purposes of things. Observation is in the service of metaphysical speculation.

Thomas was not only capable of a steadfast and logical method of arriving at the truth of things. He could also present the trend of his thought and his arguments in a clear and summary form. The theological *summa* in particular is a gem of didactic ability. His sense of the didactic is well expressed in the brief prologue: " Since the teacher of Catholic truth must instruct not only the advanced but also the beginners, according to the word of St. Paul (II Cor. 3, 1): ' As unto little ones in Christ, I gave you milk to drink, not meat ' — therefore the aim we have set for ourselves in this work is, to present the entire content of the Christian religion in such a way as to tend to the instruction of beginners. For we have observed that beginners are greatly impeded (in

[2] *Le conflit de la Morale et de la Sociologie,* 2d ed. Louvain, 1914, p. 272 ff.

[38]

their progress) by the writings of various authors, partly because of the heaping up of useless questions, articles, and arguments; partly because the knowledge necessary for beginners is not presented in a strictly methodical sequence, but in an order dictated by the explanations of books, or by the demands of disputations; and partly because the frequent repetition of the same matter causes disgust and confusion in the audience. In trying to avoid these and similar faults, we shall, trusting in God, endeavor to present the contents of the sacred science as briefly and clearly as the matter allows." The promise of these words, which indicate a clear eye for the didactic defects in the contemporary commentaries on the *Sentences* and in the *Quæstiones quodlibetales,* he fulfilled in a masterly way. The theological *summa* is a model of thorough orderliness. The arrangement into three parts, thirty-eight treatises, six hundred thirty-one questions, about three thousand articles, and ten thousand objections exhibits a remarkable constructive skill. The development of thought and argument is simple and clear. Repetitions are avoided as far as possible, superfluous questions are omitted; no explanations are made to depend on what follows later, but the best use is made of all that precedes. There is not merely system in the arrangement, an external grouping that can be viewed at a glance, but also a systematic and organic development of subject-matter that is based on inner coherence of meaning. Lacordaire compared the *summa* to the pyramids because of its majestic simplicity. The frequent comparison of it with the Gothic cathedrals of the Middle Ages is entirely justified. The more a person studies the *summa* and the more he examines its detail, the more does he admire the architectonic structure of the whole and the better does he recognize the structural laws running through the entire work.

Thomas did not only display independent power of investigation, the ripe mental energy of the logician and metaphysician, but he also knew how to make good use of the scientific results of earlier thinkers. " His mind," says Willman, " is like a lake that takes up the waters of the inflowing rivers, lets the sediment sink to the bottom, and retains a placid crystal surface, in which the blue of the sky is joyously reflected." [3] The work of Thomas shows unmistakable signs of a positivistic-historical mind. He is far removed from an apriorism that disregards all previously attained results, and spins a web of theories out of its own inner self.

Thomas had a special regard for the organic development and progress of knowledge, of profane as well as theological science, and absorbed the speculations both of the past centuries and of his own time.

[3] Willmann, *Geschichte des Idealismus*, vol. III, Braunschweig. 1907, p. 458.

In a number of passages he stressed the gradual growth of the sciences. "It lies in the nature of human reason to proceed step by step from the imperfect to the perfect. Hence we see that those occupied with the speculative sciences inherited views that were imperfect, but which were later transmitted in a more developed form. So it is also in the practical sciences" (*S. th.* I–II, q. 97, 1). Time plays an important role in the development of knowledge. "Time is, so to say, a discoverer and kind co-operator" (*In I. Eth.*, lect. 11). "We must give ear to the opinions of the ancients, no matter who it is that made the statements. There is a twofold benefit in this. We thereby acquire for our own use whatever was correctly said by them; and we avoid that in which they erred." (*In I. De anima*, lect. 2). "In establishing truth we are aided by others in two ways. We receive direct assistance from those who have already discovered truths. If every one of the earlier thinkers has found an element of truth, then these elements taken together and unified are to the later investigators a powerful help towards a comprehensive knowledge of truth. We are indirectly helped by earlier investigators in so far as their errors after diligent discussion give us the opportunity of a clearer exposition of the truth in these matters. It is therefore proper that we be grateful to all who have aided us in the pursuit of truth" (*In II. Met-*

aph., lect. 1). The opinions of earlier writers are necessary for a better knowledge of a problem and the solving of doubts. " Just as in court no judgment can be passed before the arguments for both sides are heard, so also is it necessary for the philosopher to heed the opinions and doubts of different authors in the formation of a more definitive judgment " (*In III. Metaph.*, lect. 1).

Thomas expresses his view on development and theology in the prologue to the polemic against the Greeks (*Contra errores Græcorum*): " There are two reasons for the fact that the writings of the Greek Fathers contain things that appear doubtful to modern theologians. First of all, the rise of errors in matters of faith gave the holy doctors of the Church an occasion for presenting the content of faith with greater care, in order to obviate these errors. Thus we can understand how the doctors, before the appearance of the Arian heresy, did not express themselves so exactly on the unity of the divine Essence as in the post-Arian period. The same is true in regard to other errors. We see this not only in various doctors, but also clearly in the greatest of them, Augustine. In the works that Augustine wrote after the appearance of Pelagianism, he expressed himself with much more caution on the scope of free will, than he had done in his previous works. In the latter he defended free will against the Manichæans, and made some statements which the Pelagians, deniers of divine grace, quoted in justification of their error. We should therefore not be surprised if modern theologians, writing after the existence of so many heresies, express themselves more cautiously and exactly on matters of faith in order to avoid all heresy. From this it follows that we should not readily despise or reject passages in which the ancient doctors do not express themselves so carefully as do the modern theologians. Nor should we interpret them too rigorously, but rather with reverence. The second reason for difficulties in the Greek Fathers arises from the fact that many statements sound correct in their Greek garb, but become less safe in their Latin translation, because the Latins and the Greeks use different words in defining one and the same truth of faith. Thus among the Greeks it is both correct and Catholic to say that the Father, the Son, and the Holy Ghost are three hypostases, while it would be wrong to say in Latin that they are three substances, although the Greek *hypostasis* is etymologically the same word as the Latin *substantia*. But the Latins more frequently use the word *substance* in the sense of *essence,* which the Greeks like ourselves confess to be one in God. And so, while the Greeks speak of three hypostases, we speak of three persons. There is no doubt that there are many other cases of this type.

" It is therefore the duty of a good translator to adhere faithfully to the sense, but also to be guided by the idiom of the language into which he is translating."

Thomas used the accumulated materials of former centuries and of his own time, and displayed a considerable historical sense in his method of employing his sources. He never thought of a strictly historical study as an end in itself, in the sphere of philosophy and theology. The historical knowledge of former opinions and currents of thought was for him purely a means of establishing truth. "The study of philosophy does not aim merely to find out what others have thought, but what the truth of the matter is " (*In I. De cœlo et mundo*, lect. 22). In the pursuit of this objective, he presents several surveys of the historical development of a question, but always examines it for the sake of determining the truth of the matter.

Thomas also studied sources systematically. Many of the quotations from the Fathers were, in accordance with the custom of the time and the lack of books, taken from collections of quotations, from glosses of the Sacred Scriptures, the Decretum of Gratian, the decretals, and the works of former theologians. In the dedication of his *Catena aurea* (on Matthew) to Urban IV, he acknowledges that he is indebted to the glosses for quotations from the Fathers. But he also made systematic studies of texts, notably in philosophy and in patristics. An anecdote in the acts of canonization indicated his desire for the complete works of the Fathers. "One day as Brother Thomas was returning to Paris from St. Denis with several confreres, and the panorama of the city spread out before them, one of the companions said to Thomas: ' Father, how beautiful is this city of Paris! ' Brother Thomas answered: ' Indeed, very beautiful.' The other continued: ' If only this city were yours! '. To which Thomas answered: ' What should I do with it? ' — ' You could sell it to the King of France, and build Dominican convents with the proceeds.' — ' In all truth,' Thomas replied, ' I should rather have St. Chrysostom's homilies on Matthew.' " Montfaucon, editor of the works of St. Chrysostom, considered this remark highly creditable to Thomas. The manuscripts at Paris must have served Thomas well in his study of sources. St. Louis had erected a library adjacent to the Saint Chapelle, out of which Vincent of Beauvais gathered the materials for his famous encyclopedia of learning (the *Speculum magnum*). The libraries of Notre Dame and St. Victor likewise contained considerable materials. At the papal court, the growing collection of manuscripts in possession of the popes was at the disposal of Thomas. But as to details, for instance, it is impossible to determine in which libraries

Thomas gathered the quotations from twenty-three Latin and fifty-seven Greek Fathers for his *Catena aurea.*

In the use of these sources Thomas also showed a sense of historical criticism. The text he used was by no means a matter of indifference to him. For his study of Aristotle he was not satisfied with the Latin versions from the Arabian. He induced his linguistic confrere and friend, William of Moerbeke, to undertake a faithful Latin translation of the physical, metaphysical, and ethical writings of Aristotle directly out of the Greek original, so that he might have a reliable text for his commentaries. We may hold that Thomas himself had some knowledge of Greek. In patristic literature he likewise sought proper texts. In the dedication to Urban IV of his *catena* on Matthew, he complains of the *vicious translation* of Chrysostom, and says he could often give only the sense and not the exact words of passages because of the defective text. In the dedication of his *catena* on Mark to Cardinal Hannibaldus, he points out that he had taken care to have the Greek text translated into reliable Latin. Again Thomas makes many a happy decision in solving questions of authenticity, thus indicating a sound critical sense, which merited the praise of the Maurists and of Angelo Mais. A few indications will be given here. Thomas declared the treatise *De infantia Salvatoris* to be apocryphal (*S. th.* III, q. 36, a. 4 ad 3; q. 43, a. 3 ad 1). He correctly assigned to Gennadius the book *De ecclesiasticis dogmatis* imputed to Augustine (*Quodl.* VI, 10). Similarly he denied to Augustine the works *De mirabilibus sacræ Scripturæ* (*S. th.* III, q. 45, a. 3 ad 2) and *De spiritu et anima* (*De anima*, 12 ad 1). He intimated that a Cistercian monk might be the author of the latter; and the Maurists actually attribute it to the Cistercian Alcher of Clairvaux. Again he denied the authenticity of the *De unitate et uno*, which had been attributed to Boethius, and pointed out the divergent character of its style (*De spiritualibus creaturis* 3, ad 9). His most important critical achievement is his judgment on the origin of the *Liber de causis*. He considered it an excerpt from the *Institutio theologica* of Proclus. " No one in the Middle Ages spoke of the origin of the *Liber de causis* so clearly as Thomas." [4]

Thomas approaches his sources with sympathy, but with independent judgment. He esteems Aristotle very highly. Nevertheless he goes his own way in questions which according to his conviction are not correctly solved by the Stagirite. Thus (*S. th.* I, q. 46, a. 1) he departs from the Aristotelian position of the eternity of creation, but adds the remark that Aristotle had intended to give only a dialectical proof for this thesis, not an apodictical one.

[4] Cl. Baeumker, *Witelo*. Muenster, 1908, p. 189.

Thomas is more severe with the Arabian and Jewish philosophers, especially Averroes and Avencebrol. The treatise *De unitate intellectus contra Averroistas*, against Siger of Brabant, is based on an examination of Averroes' conception of Aristotle, that is strictly objective and independent. The monograph *De substantiis separatis* is a very thorough and objective exposition of his differences with Avencebrol. Thomas treats the Church Fathers with great reverence, whence Cardinal Cajetan says of him: "Because he showed the greatest respect for the Fathers of the Church, he was, as it were, endowed with the profundity of all " (*In S. th.* II–II, q. 148, a. 4). But Thomas never loses his independent judgment by reason of his respect and modesty. Wherever he departs from the Fathers, he does so with forbearance. Thus he says (*De pot.* q. 3, a. 18): "As this is the opinion of great teachers, of Basil, of Gregory Nazianzen, and others, it is not to be condemned as erroneous." In regard to Augustine, whom he considered the greatest of the Church Fathers, he likewise retains his independence. This is evident especially in questions of psychology and epistemology, in which he seeks his solutions in accordance with the method pointed out by Aristotle. Citations from Augustine are less frequent here. The opposition between Augustine and Aristotle is levelled down as much as possible, by doubting the apodictical char-

acter of the Augustinian statements, pointing to the
Platonic viewpoint of the great Church Father, and
bringing the exuberant spiritualism back to a more
moderate position. Often Augustine is quoted by
occasion of mentioning the opinions of others, or of
stating the problem. The Franciscan reaction to the
views of Thomas is strict evidence of the fact that
Thomas' position in regard to Augustine was considered an independent one by his contemporaries.

The third characteristic of Thomas' life and labor
is the ethico-religious foundation, which never became obtrusive, and therefore shines forth the more
effectively out of his writings. " A sacred mood,"
writes Eucken,[5] " pervades throughout. As in a gigantic cathedral, we go from the vestibule of the
world to the sanctuary in expectation of the all-holy.
The lower contains implicitly a desire for the higher,
and strengthens this desire by mysterious signs and
presentiments. The entire series of purposes finally
points to the one goal of divine glory. Erudition
takes on the appearance of a service in the temple."
This religious atmosphere reveals itself primarily
in the longing for ever deeper knowledge of God.
The question, " What is God? " is the motto and the
motive of the scientific labors of his life. " We know
of God that He exists, is the cause of all being, and is

[5] Eucken, *Die Philosophie des Thomas von Aquin und die Kultur der Neuzeit.* Bad Sachsa, 1910, p. 15.

infinitely higher than all else. This is the ultimate peak of our knowledge here on earth " (*Contra gentes* III, 49). In his desire for knowledge of God, Thomas was gratefully happy to receive the teaching of Christian revelation on the nature and life of God. " Not one of the pre-Christian philosophers," he said in his explanation of the Apostolic Creed, " could with all his power of thought know so much about God as a simple woman since the advent of Christ knows through faith." This firm devotion to the contents of supernatural revelation explains Thomas' reverential attitude towards the Church, in which he saw the mediator and guardian of revealed truth. " The practice of the Church possesses the highest authority, and we must be directed by it in all things. Even the doctrine of the Catholic teachers has its authority from the Church. Hence we must hold the custom of the Church in higher esteem than the authority of an Augustine or a Jerome " (*Quodlib.* II, a. 7). He is ever intent upon being true to the teaching and the spirit of the Church. For the authority of the Pope he shows the highest respect. His admiration for the Christian antiquity is glowing — " Christian antiquity, the flourishing age of a warm Christian faith " (*S. th.* III, q. 80, a. 10 ad 5).

The keen desire for knowledge of God also had its effect on his efforts toward a virtuous life. Moral purity and holiness he considers a valuable aid to the fathoming of divine truths and mysteries. The high ideal embraced by Thomas in this regard is evident from a letter to the novice Friar John, who had asked him for advice on a good method of study and acquiring knowledge: " Since you have asked me in Christ, dear John, to tell you how you must study for the attainment of a treasury of knowledge, I shall mention the following points of advice. Prefer to arrive at knowledge over small streamlets, and do not plunge immediately into the ocean (of wisdom), since progress must go from the easier to the more difficult. That is my admonition and your instruction. I exhort you to be chary of speech, and to go into the conversation room sparingly. Take great heed of the purity of your conscience. Never cease the practice of prayer. Love to be diligent in your cell, if you would be led to the wine cellar of wisdom. Ever be loving towards all. Do not bother yourself about the doings of others. Nor be too familiar with anyone, since too great familiarity breeds contempt and easily leads away from study. Do not engage in the doings and conversations of the worldly. Above all shun roaming about outside the monastery. Do not fail to walk in the footsteps of the saintly and the good. Do not consider from whom you hear anything, but impress upon your memory everything good that is said. Make an effort to understand thoroughly whatever you read

[51]

and hear. In all doubts seek to penetrate to the truth. Try always to store away as much as possible in the chambers of your mind. What is too far above you, do not now strive after. If you follow these directions you will produce useful blossoms and fruits in the vineyard of the Lord of Hosts, as long as you live. If you do all this, you will attain what you desire. Farewell." This letter contains some valuable hints on method, and in particular some splendid ideas on the relation between moral purity of heart and true knowledge. We here find exhortations and ideas that were later voiced with such impressive simplicity by Thomas à Kempis in the *Imitation of Christ*.

It may have been greatly because of the ethico-religious bent in Thomas and his writings, that the later German mysticism, inspired also by Albert the Great, attached itself so intimately to him. In the *Summa theologica* (II–II, qq. 179–182), the mystics found the profoundest and the clearest exposition of the contemplative life. Tauler frequently refers to Master Thomas. Henry Suso calls his guide " the clear light, beloved St. Thomas the teacher." The newly found commentary on the *Sentences* by the mystic John of Sterngassen is an illuminating introduction into Thomistic speculation.

CHAPTER IV

THE SOURCES OF THOMISTIC THOUGHT

HE range of sources drawn upon by Thomas is astounding, especially if we take into consideration the means and the conditions of mental research existing at this time.

In philosophy Thomas shows a better knowledge of Aristotle than any other person in the Middle Ages. He wrote commentaries on the greater and most important part of Aristotle's works, using the reliable translation of William of Moerbeke as a basis. As Bartholomew of Lucca said, his commentaries were "in a very individual and new manner of interpretation." They aimed at a clear, summary exposition of the complicated theories of the Stagirite. In Scholastic circles Thomas was designated as *the* expositor (i.e. of Aristotle), for instance, by Giles of Rome, Henry Bate, etc. Moderns like Ch. Jourdain, Fr. Brentano, G. v. Hertling, and others, have esteemed his method of commenting very highly. His own systematic works, large as well as small, philosophical and theological, show a rare acquaintance with the works of the Philosopher (Aristotle). Thomas knew Plato chiefly through the critical references to him in Aristotle, but was thereby not deterred from taking up into his system the theory of ideas as interpreted by Augustine. He frequently cites the Greek commentators of Aristotle, Porphyry, Themistius, Simplicius, Alexander of Aphrodisias. Boethius, the last Roman and first Scholastic, is frequently used. Thomas was also well acquainted with the Arabian and Jewish philosophy, and was a sharp judge of its lights and shadows. He seemed to esteem Avicenna more highly than Averroes. He explained his points of disagreement with the *Fons vitæ* of Avencebrol more than once. The *More Nebuchim* of Moses Maimonides was to him a familiar book.

Of Neoplatonic writings, apart from theological sources (Pseudo-Dionysius), the *Liber de causis* and after 1268 the " *Theological Elements* " (Στοιχειω-σις Θεολογική) of Proclus (in the translation of William of Moerbeke) were available to him. He also knew and cited the treatise *De intelligentiis,* which was Neoplatonic in tendency.

In theology, Thomas displayed an extraordinary familiarity with the entire Scriptures, which he seems to have quoted by heart very often. He made good use of the biblical glosses of Walafrid Strabo and

Anselm of Laon. Especially numerous are his quotations from the Fathers. Besides the patristic works
that were readily available to his contemporaries
(Ambrose, Augustine, Jerome, John Damascene,
Pseudo-Dionysius, Hilary of Poitiers, Gregory the
Great, Isidore of Seville, etc.), his later writings show
an intimate knowledge of St. John Chrysostom, and
St. Cyril of Alexandria, which knowledge consider-
ably influenced his Christology and his sacramental-
ism. Of the earlier Scholastics he knows and cites
Anselm of Canterbury, Rupert of Deutz, Bernard of
Clairvaux, Gilbert de la Porrée, Hugh of St. Victor,
whom he esteems highly, Richard of St. Victor,
Joachim of Flora. Nor were Abelard and Alain de
Lille unknown to him. But the most frequently
quoted author of this period is naturally the *Magister
Sententiarum,* Peter the Lombard, who, however,
must submit to more than occasional correction.

In accordance with the custom of his day, Thomas
referred to theologians of the thirteenth century by
means of the *quidam* — " a certain one." He mentions only *Præpositinus* and *William of Auxerre* by
name, both of whom were at Paris in the first third
of the century, and wrote *summæ.* The various persons referred to by the *quidam* can be identified only
after the unprinted pre-Thomistic literature is well
known, and after the relation of Thomas to the
printed sources, to Alexander of Hales, Albert the

Great, Bonaventure, has been established in detail. As in Scholastic tradition a great number of views, questions, and objections were passed on from generation to generation, it will often be very difficult to determine the identity of the *quidam*. We may remark, by the way, that there is evidence for Thomas' employment of the unprinted *summa* of Robert of Melun (d. 1167) and of the *Sentences* of Peter of Poitiers (d. 1205).

Thomas also possessed a thorough knowledge of the older conciliar decisions, as we can see particularly from his Christology. His knowledge of canon law, which is evident from the frequent citation of Gratian and the decretals, exceeds that of the majority of doctors of his time. In his day canon law and theology were accepted as two distinct disciplines and faculties. Occasionally Thomas also quotes from Roman law. Finally he not infrequently intersperses his expositions with passages from the ancient classics, also the poets. In fact, quotations from Horace, Ovid, Cæsar, Cicero, Seneca, Terence, Sallust, Livy, Strabo, Valerius Maximus, and the like, give a humanistic atmosphere to the source materials used by Thomas.

CHAPTER V

THE STRUGGLE FOR LEADERSHIP IN SCHOLASTIC
THOUGHT

T WAS a premature death that
ended the tireless scientific labors of
Thomas. An Oxford manuscript of
the *Summa theologica* (Balliol College 44, s. XIV) contains the remark:
" Here Thomas dies. O Death, how
thou art accursed! " But the product of his energy
has outlived the great theologian, and has given him
a leading position in the intellectual life of the Catholic Church. His views indeed met with opposition
immediately after his death; and they had to go
through many a battle before they established themselves definitely. It is quite contrary to historical
truth to speak as if the views of Thomas had been
incontestably accepted by his own order or by Scholastics in general shortly after his death.

The opposition of the conservative Augustinian
tendency to the Aristotelianism of Thomas, which
had already embittered his last stay at Paris, became

[57]

acute soon after his death. On March 7, 1277, Bishop
Stephen Tempier of Paris condemned 219 propositions, among them the theory of Thomas on the principle of individuation. On March 18 of the same
year Archbishop Robert Kilwardby, a theologian
of renown, who represented a circle of learned Dominicans quite out of sympathy with the Aristotelianism of Albert the Great and Thomas, put some of
Thomas' statements into the list of proscribed propositions. But the most severe opponent of Thomas
among the Dominicans of the first decades of the
fourteenth century was Durandus of St. Pourçain
(d. 1332).

During his last stay at Paris Thomas had had differences with the Franciscan theologians. Mention
was already made of the attack by John Peckham on
the Aristotelianism of Thomas. Matthew of Aquasparta (d. 1302), pupil of Bonaventure, takes ex-
ception in his *Quæstiones disputatæ* to various points
of Thomas' teaching. This opposition between the
Franciscan Augustinianism and the Aristotelianism
of Thomas was continued with increased vehemence
in the conflict between Scotists and Thomists. William of Ware is the connecting link between the older
Franciscan school and Duns Scotus. Soon after him
came the two most important Franciscan critics of the
Thomistic doctrines, Duns Scotus (d. 1308) and
William de la Mare (in Oxford ca. 1285). The

latter, not long after the death of Thomas, put together a long list of points of difference between Thomas and the Franciscans in his *Correctorium fratris Thomæ* (Polemic against Thomas). When the disciples of Thomas produced counter-treatises, another Franciscan, as indicated in a Berlin manuscript, composed a second tract defending the points of attack that had been made against Thomas.

The latter's doctrine also found important opponents in the ranks of the secular clergy who taught theology, in particular Henry of Ghent (d. 1293). Even Godfrey of Fontaines (d. after 1306), who gives the highest praise to Thomas, opposes many of his views. From this condition it is evident, that the Thomistic philosophy had to overcome numerous difficulties, before it could arrive at a position of leadership in the Dominican order, and still more so, in the learned circles outside the latter. The acuteness of the situation is seen strikingly from the well-authenticated fact, that Albert the Great did not shun setting out on foot from Cologne to Paris in his old age, in order to defend the doctrines of his recently deceased, famous disciple.

The difficulties raised against Thomism, however, were successfully vanquished. The friends and disciples of Thomas were specially active in setting up a strong defence against the manifold opposition. Thomas had drawn a large number of disciples to his views; and after his death they defended their scientific heritage valiantly. In miniatures and manuscripts, and in a panel painting in the academy of Florence (of the school of Fiesole), the school of St. Thomas is depicted. Numerous disciples, Dominicans and others, are listening intently to his words. It is, in fact, a good illustration for the following words of the reliable biographer of Thomas, Peter Calo (ca. 1320): "When Thomas had taken up his work as teacher, and had begun the disputations and lectures, such a multitude of pupils flocked to his school, that the lecture room could hardly contain all who were attracted by the word of so renowned a master and inspired by him to progress in the pursuit of learning. Under the light of his teaching many masters flourished, both of the Dominicans and of the secular clergy. The reason for this was the synthetic, clear, and intelligible method of his lectures." [1] If we are to mention the most noteworthy of the disciples and followers who represented and defended his views, we must begin with the Augustinian theologians Giles of Rome (d. 1316), Augustinus Triumphus of Ancona (d. 1328), and James Capocci of Viterbo (d. 1307). The Carmelite general, Gerard of Bologna (d. 1317), whose unpublished theological *summa* shows so many points of

---

[1] *Vita S. Thomæ Aquinatis auctore Petro Calo.* Ed. D. Pruemmer. Tolosæ, 1911, p. 30.

[60]

contact with the masterpiece of Thomas, seems to have sat at the latter's feet. Among the professors of the secular clergy Peter of Auvergne (d. 1305) was an enthusiastic disciple, who completed the unfinished commentaries of his master on Aristotle.

Among the Dominicans there were naturally many faithful disciples and friends, enthusiastic followers, who studied his writings, explained his teaching, developed it further, and preserved and defended it as a precious treasure. The works of Thomas were used in the schools of his order at an early date. This is evident from the numerous manuscripts, excerpts, abridgments, tables, concordances, etc., by means of which his works were made more available for purposes of instruction, and more accessible for ready study. A Paris manuscript, containing an abridgment (*Abbreviatio*) of the *Secunda secundæ* (a part of the *Summa theologica*) from the pen of the Dominican Galienus de Oyto, dates from 1288. Of the most faithful Dominican disciples and followers, the Italians, John of Cajatia, Reginald of Piperno, Peter of Andria, and Bartholomew of Lucca (d. 1327), have left touching expressions of their attachment. The last three continued incomplete works of Thomas. Bartholomew of Lucca, famous as a Church historian, whose Hexaëmeron is proof of his thorough knowledge of the psychology of his master, says of the latter: " Thomas excels all modern doctors in philosophy and in theology, as is generally recognized; and he is therefore today called the *Doctor communis* (universally known and recognized) at the University of Paris." Similar testimonies and enthusiasm are found among other disciples of the great theologian. An enthusiastic follower, who further developed the Thomistic epistemology in particular, is Bernard of Trilia (d. 1292). Another admiring disciple of Thomas was Remigio de Girolami (d. 1319), who, as the teacher of Dante, acquainted the great poet with the Thomistic synthesis.

Of special interest are the Dominican theologians who defended the views of their teacher against the attacks of the opponents. Giles of Lessines in a special treatise (*De unitate formæ*), defended the Thomistic position on the unity of substantial form against Robert Kilwardby, May 1278, and thus publicly took his stand in opposition to the condemnation of Oxford. Against the condemnation by the Bishop of Paris, Stephen Tempier, Thomas was defended by John of Naples (d. ca. 1325), whose treatises are still unpublished. The *Correctorium fratris Thomæ* of the Franciscan William de la Mare was answered point for point by a number of disciples in a series of counter-tracts entitled: *Correctorium corruptorii fratris Thomæ* (Correction of the distortion of Brother Thomas). Most of this controversial literature, generally anonymous, has been sifted only recently. One of the tracts against William de la Mare was published under the name of Giles of Rome. It was probably the work of Richard Clapwell. The *Correctorium corruptorii fratris Thomæ* of John Quidort of Paris (d. 1306) is preserved in several manuscript copies. Further defences were composed by Ramberto de Primadizzi and John of Parma. Thomas was also defended against other opponents by his faithful followers. Bernard of Clermont (d. after 1303) defended his teacher against Henry of Ghent, Godrey of Fontaines, and even against Giles of Rome. Similar defences of Thomistic views, which have apparently been lost, were written by the Englishmen Robert of Hereford and William of Macclesfield. An enthusiastic defender and a reliable interpreter of Thomas was Thomas of Sutton, likewise an Englishman. Besides the Neoplatonic tendency represented by Ulric of Strasburg, Dietrich of Freiburg, Master Eckhart and Berthold of Moosburg, there is evidence of a powerful and rigorously Thomistic trend among the Dominicans of the German lands. Of those living at the end of the thirteenth and the beginning of the fourteenth centuries, I may mention the three mystics, John of Sterngassen, Gerard of Sterngassen and Nicholas of Strasburg — of all of whom I have discovered extensive Latin writings, Thomistic in spirit — and John Piccardi of Lichtenberg and Henry of Lübeck.

The most important adherent and defender of Thomism at the beginning of the fourteenth century is Hervæus of Nedellec (Hervæus Natalis, d. 1323), indirectly a pupil of Thomas, who as General of the Dominicans promoted and witnessed the latter's canonization. A large part of his writings, mainly unpublished, is devoted to the defence of Thomas against Henry of Ghent, Duns Scotus, Durandus, Aureolus, Godfrey of Fontaines, etc. He was undoubtedly very influential in giving a recognized position to the system of Aquinas, not only as the accepted teaching within the order, but also as the most important general Scholastic synthesis. Another influential Thomist of the fourteenth century was Peter de Palude (d. 1342), who frequently mentions " doctor noster frater Thomas " (our teacher brother Thomas). Against the attacks of Durandus of St. Pourçain a defence was written by Durandus of Aurillac (d. 1380). But the most comprehensive, decisive, and thorough defence is that of John Capreolus (d. 1444), the " prince of Thomists." His *Defensiones theologiæ divi Thomæ Aquinatis* (Defence of the theology of the saintly Thomas Aquinas) gives us the first general codification of the teachings of Aquinas, and constitute a general defence against the opponents of Thomistic thought (especially Duns Scotus, Aureolus, Durandus, Occam, Gregory of Rimini).

Gradually, therefore, the teaching of Thomas was accorded the position and the respect that it deserved by reason of its inner value, not only within the Dominican ranks but also outside. Besides the endeavors of followers, which we have here described, this was due to the energetic action of the Dominicans both at their general chapters and at their provincial gatherings. A few indications will suffice. The general chapter at Milan in 1278 sent two lectors to England, that they might proceed rigorously against the brothers who were there opposing the writings of Brother Thomas. Similar resolutions and measures were repeated at the general chapters of Paris, in 1279 and 1286. The general chapter at Saragossa in 1309 designated the teaching of Thomas as the norm for the studies of the order. The general chapter at Metz in 1313 designated "the teaching of the venerable doctor Brother Thomas of Aquin" *sanior et communior*, "the sounder and more common teaching," and ordained that no Dominican should be sent to Paris for any academic degrees until he had studied Thomas three years. Such regulations and laudations were increased at the general chapters of Bologna, 1315 and 1329, Carcassonne 1342, and Madrid 1346. Similar action was taken at the provincial chapters. Thus at the gathering of the Roman province of Arezzo in 1315, to mention but one, a Brother Ubertus Guidi was suspended from teaching for two years and condemned to a ten days' fast on water and bread because he had spoken against Thomas. It need hardly be remarked that these events, extending into the middle of the fourteenth century, gave Thomism the leading position within the Dominican order.

Finally, another very important factor in the victory of Thomism was the intervention of the popes in favor of Thomas. The most important act of the highest authority of the Church was his canonization by Pope John XXII, July 18, 1323. "He wrought as many miracles as he wrote articles," said the Pope on that occasion. An immediate consequence of the canonization undoubtedly was the act of Bishop Stephen de Borreto of Paris, February 14, 1424, retracting the condemnation of Thomistic propositions passed by his predecessor Stephen Tempier on March 7, 1277. In 1327 John XXII commissioned the Dominican William Dulcini to undertake a more exact compilation of the writings of Thomas.

The successors of John XXII up to the present time have honored and protected the person and the teaching of Thomas. A description of the history of Thomistic theories down to our own day is beyond the scope of this enterprise. "The fate of the theological *summa* was that of ecclesiastical learning." [2] We are concerned only with presenting the struggles

[2] Fr. Ehrle, *Stimmen aus Maria Laach*, XVIII, p. 298.

and difficulties which Thomas' views had to en-
counter after his death before establishing themselves
definitely.

It may be worthy of remark, that at the close of
the Middle Ages Thomas enjoyed esteem also in
Byzantine theology. His *Summa theologica,* the
Summa contra gentes, his commentaries on Aristotle's psychology and physics, and various smaller
works, were translated into the Greek by Georgios
Scholarios, Demetrios Kydones, and others. The library of Athos, the Ambrosian Library of Milan,
and the Laurentian Library of Florence, the library
of St. Mark's in Venice, and especially the Vatican
library, contain a number of such manuscripts. Demetrios Kydones even left a letter in which he presents a methodical instruction on the study of the
theology of Thomas, and a convincing defence of
the latter against Nilus Kabasilas. Very recently attention has also been directed to Armenian translations of Thomas.

PART TWO
The Thomistic Synthesis

CHAPTER VI

THOUGHT AND BEING.   FAITH AND KNOWLEDGE

HE foundations on which the gigantic edifice of Thomistic synthesis is erected are formed of a twofold conviction. The deepest foundation is the conviction that our thought can know and attain being, the realm of essences, causes, purposes, and laws, that lies beyond the world of appearances. It is a conviction of the reality and the knowability of the supersensory order, a definite adherence to the possibility and reality of metaphysics.

The second foundation of the Thomistic system is the firm conviction that over and beyond the scope of the supersensory, of the metaphysical, which is accessible to natural thought, there is an endless horizon of the supernatural, of the Christian mysteries revealed by God, a horizon that is even here on earth opened to man by means of the light of faith.

At the beginning of this exposition, therefore, it is necessary to give a brief account of the principles of St. Thomas on the question of *Thought and Being* and of *Faith and Knowledge.*

1. *Thought and Being*

Thomas was ever metaphysical in his thought. The profound grasp, the development, and the comprehensive employment of the metaphysics of Aristotle, also for a better understanding of theological truths, is his great achievement. His teacher Albert the Great paved the way for him in this respect. · E. Rolfes calls Thomas Aquinas " the best commentator of the Aristotelian metaphysics, that we have." Thomas' metaphysical genius pervades his great systematic works. It reveals itself particularly in his treatises on God, and shows itself even amidst the more strictly theological treatises on grace, on the Incarnation, and on the sacraments. As perfect miniatures of his metaphysical powers we have many smaller monographs; for instance, the profound treatise *De ente et essentia.* It is probably not by mere accident that metaphysical problems were preferably treated by his disciples. Only a few central points of his theory of being can be emphasized here, those that are of special importance for his complete synthesis. We shall meet with his metaphysical prin-

ciples again and again in his teaching on God and creation, in his psychology and ethics.

*Objectivity of Human Thought. Justification of
Metaphysics.* " Some persons have upheld the opinion that our knowing powers know only their own
modifications, that the senses, for instance, perceive
nothing but the alteration, the stimulation of their
own organs. Accordingly the intellect likewise
knows only its own subjective modifications, that is,
the intelligible species, the concept taken up by it.
Hence these species are both object and content of
intellectual knowledge, a merely subjective modification of the intellect.

" But this view must be rejected for two reasons.
First of all, that which we know intellectually and
that of which the branches of knowledge treat are
one and the same. If then our thought could attain
only what is merely subjective, the species in the
mind, the sciences could not refer to any objects existing beyond the mind. Their entire scope would be
limited to these subjective, intellectual concepts.
Secondly, from such a subjective interpretation of human knowledge, it would follow that all we are conscious of is true, and that two contradictory statements would both be true at the same time. For if
the mind knows only its own subjective determinations, then it can judge only about these. The subjective modification is then the only norm of the

content of a judgment. Hence every judgment would have the same claim to truth. For instance, if taste perceives only its own modification, then he who has a normal healthy sense of taste will judge: Honey is sweet — and his judgment would be true. He who has his sense of taste already affected will judge: Honey is sour — and his judgment would be equally true on the above supposition. Each one would here judge according to the condition of his sense of taste. As a consequence of this one-sided subjective interpretation of human knowledge, according to which the subjective concept, the intelligible species, is the object of intellectual knowledge, all difference between the true and the false would vanish.

" These two unacceptable consequences, the denial of the objective, real character and value of knowledge, and the disappearance of all distinction of true and false, of yes and no, justify us, nay force us to adhere to the objectivity of our knowledge and thought, and to realize that the intelligible species, the subjective impressions and determinations of our intellect, are not the direct objects, the contents of our thought. These mental forms are rather the means through which we are led to a knowledge of the reality external to us. The intelligible species are subjective forms that determine our intellect to a knowledge of the objective reality. That of which we are primarily aware is the external object, of which the species is a mental sign. Only secondarily can we speak of the intelligible species as a content of thought, in so far as the mind is reflexly active and contemplates its own activity and thus also the species as principle of this activity." (*S. th.* I, q. 85, a. 2.) Thus our minds attain objective reality, reach out beyond the confines of the subjective.

The Subjective Character of Human Thought. Thus does Thomas construct his bridge from thought to being, from subject to object. Outside our minds there is a reality corresponding to our intellectual concepts, a reality forming the essence and core of the things and activities of the world of appearances perceived by the senses. Our concepts of the essences of things, of laws and purposes, causes and effects, are not mere subjective fictions, but signify the grasping, on the part of thought, of a reality that lies outside us. In the relation of the content of our act of thought to this reality consists the truth of our intellectual knowledge.

Still, according to Thomas, this character of truth and of the real in our thought in no way demands that there be a mechanical similarity between the manner of knowing and the manner of being of the object: " The intellect knows things not according to the manner of being they have in themselves, but according to its own nature. The material objects,

which are below the level of our intellect in their
being, are in our thought in a simpler manner than
they are in themselves. On the other hand our intellect knows pure spiritual substances, which are
above the level of our thought, not according to the
simple manner of their being, but in the manner in
which it knows compound things " (*S. th.* I, q. 50,
a. 2).

General Concepts. Awareness of the subjective
element in our intellectual concepts enables Thomas
to find the right position between a nominalism that
denies all value to universals and an extreme realism
that objectifies the universal as such: " That which
we designate by names can be divided into three
classes. The first class comprises those things that
are outside the mind in their entire being, e.g., the
man, the stone. The second class is formed of the
things that exist only in our mind, as dreams, image
of a chimera, etc. To the third class belong those
things that have a foundation in the reality outside
the mind, but receive their own formal character from
the activity of the mind. Such are the general concepts. ' Humanity ' is something in the realm of
reality, but it is not real in its formal universality.
For in reality there is no one general, abstract ' humanity ' common to many. The character of universality is given to the concept ' humanity ' by our
mind. By means of the activity of our intellect ' hu-

manity' gets the logical relation (*intentio*) through which it appears as a class concept. The same is true of the concept of time. This concept has a real foundation in motion, in the before and after of motion; but the formal element in time, the measuring by number, is the product of the numbering activity of our intellect" (*In I Sent.* d. 19, q. 5, a. 1). Thus Thomas clearly distinguishes between the content, the actual core of the universal concept, to which something real outside our minds corresponds, and the form of the universal and the abstract, which is a product of our thought.

The Meanings of Being. Thomas set forth the meanings of being with inimitable brevity and clearness (*De veritate* I, 1), thereby giving the simplest expression to his whole teaching on being. " Just as in demonstrative proof we must finally come down to some self-evident principles (not capable of or in need of proof), so too in the search for the essence of anything. For else we should in both cases be obliged to proceed indefinitely, and consequently all science and all knowledge of things would be impossible. But that which our intellect attains primarily as the best known, and into which it resolves all its concepts, is being, as Avicenna explains at the beginning of his *Metaphysics*. It is therefore necessary that we acquire all other intellectual concepts by addition to being. But nothing can be added to be-

ing, that is of a different nature (from being), such
as holds for the difference added to the genus, or the
accident to the substance; for every nature is essentially a being, something that is. For this reason
Aristotle shows in the third book of his *Metaphysics*
that being cannot be a class name. But we can speak
of the addition of something to being in this way,
that what we add to being expresses a mode of being
that is not explicitly indicated by the term *being*.
This may happen in two ways: First of all, the expressed mode of being may be any special mode of
being. For there are different grades of being, in
accordance with which we speak of different modes of
being. According to these modes of being we distinguish the different genera (categories) of things.
Substance does not add a difference to being such as
would imply a nature superadded to being. The
term *substance* rather expresses a certain definite
mode of being, namely that of being-in-itself (*per
se ens*). The same holds of the other categories.
Secondly, the expressed mode may be a determination that is true in general of all being. And this
mode again can be viewed in two ways: First, in so
far as it is found *per se* in every being; and secondly,
in so far as it is found in every being in relation to
another. The mode found in every being *per se* is
either an affirmation or a negation in the thing. Now
there is only one thing that can be affirmed absolutely

[75]

and that can be accepted for every being, and that is its essence (*essentia*). In this sense we use the term *thing* (*res*). This word *thing* (*res*) is distinguished from being in this that being (*ens*) expresses the act of being (existing), while thing (*res*) expresses the essence (*quiditas sive essentia*). The negation which is absolutely found in all things is the absence of division (*indivisio*). This is expressed by the term *one* (*unum*), for the one is nothing but the undivided being. If we further examine the modes of being existing in all things, in the second aspect mentioned above, i.e., as the mode existing in any thing in its relation to another, we again have a twofold view: First, in so far as a thing is distinct from another; and this is expressed by the term *something* (*aliquid*), for something means, so to say, another thing. As being is said to be one in so far as it is undivided in itself, so it is called something, a single thing, in so far as it is distinct from others. Secondly, in so far as a thing is identical with another; and that is not conceivable unless we have something that is capable of being identical with all that is. Now we have just that in the soul, which according to Aristotle is in a way all things. In the soul there is the power of knowing and willing. The thing as object of the tendency of will is designated by the term *good*. The good is, as Aristotle says at the beginning of his *Nichomachean Ethics*, what all strive for. The thing as object of the intellect is expressed by the term *true.*"

The Highest Principles of Thought and Being. Intimately connected with the derivation of the different meanings of being, with this insight into the basic roots of metaphysics, is Thomas' theory of the highest principles of thought and being. " In everything known by the mind of man order reigns. What is known first by our intellect is being. Intellectual grasp of being is included in every thought of man. Thence we have the first indemonstrable principle, that we cannot at once both affirm and deny a thing. This principle rests on the concept of being and of non-being and is the primary basis for all other principles " (*S. th.* I–II, q. 94, a. 2). This principle consequently has two characteristics: On the one hand, objective validity, since it is based on the concept of being and non-being. It is at the same time a principle of thought and of being. On the other hand, it is indemonstrable, since it cannot be led back to a higher principle and is at the same time the support and the point of departure for all demonstration, since the other supreme laws of being and thought can without difficulty be led back to it, and finally since all demonstration must ultimately stop at this principle as in its first norm.

The Reality of Substances. A fundamental truth of the Thomistic theory of being is the conviction of the reality of substances. There exist firm, self-dependent things, subjects of the actions, motions, activities, changes, such as we perceive in the world about us. There is in ourselves an enduring principle, the basis and root of all the phenomena of our mental and bodily life, the substantial soul.[1] The supreme substance is God, creator of all other substances. "Substance is a thing, whose essence it is, not to have its being in another thing; accident is a thing, whose nature it is to be in another" (*Quodl.* IX, a. 5 ad 2). The character of not having its being in another thing, of having being on its own account, self-subsistence, is the primary and essential element in the notion of substance. This element is true of God in the most eminent degree. The character of being the possessor of accidents, or of having also that which is not self-subsisting, is the secondary element of the notion of substance, found only in the concept of created substances.

Like Aristotle, Thomas distinguishes a first substance, the real concrete individual being (Socrates), and a second substance, the essence of the individual being (humanity). For him there was no occasion for attacking theories that are common today, such

[1] It may not be superfluous to remark that almost all of the non-Thomistic definitions of substance and soul met with today are little more than caricatures of the Thomistic concept. The soul is for the Scholastic essentially a self-moving principle — a notion that for the Scholastic is also highly expressive of what is today often referred to as a vital urge, *élan vital*, tendency to develop, etc. — Tr.

as that of actualism or phenomenalism, which deny the reality of a body or a soul substance, and try to resolve reality into motions, actions, representations, phenomena without a firm substantial basis. But he showed the way to various proofs of the reality of substances, and, as we shall see, emphasized the real distinction between the substance of the soul and its powers more sharply than the other Scholastics, and attributed the phenomena of mental life to the substance of the soul. From the becoming and the action of things he concludes the existence of substances, and is convinced that the world would be mere appearance and not reality, if all were motion, and there were no permanent enduring being. He is so convinced of the reality of substances, that it is precisely to the substances, things existing in themselves, he attributes being in the proper and truest sense of the term (*S. th.* I, q. 90, a. 2).

Substantial being, being-in-and-for-itself, has various degrees of perfection. An individual substance, independent and self-sufficient and incommunicable, is called a suppositum or hypostasis. If this hypostasis is a rational being, it is called a person. Hence the concept of person gives us the highest form of being-in-itself, of possessing one's own being. By the possession of reason the independence of the hypostasis is increased. For it is by means of reason, self-consciousness, that the intellectual substance shows itself a self-dependent being, existing-for-itself, the subject of free actions, of rights and duties. "As it is proper to a substance to exist in itself, so is it also capable of acting by itself. For action follows the nature of a thing. And the power of acting by itself, of independent action (*per se agere*), exists in a more excellent manner in a substance endowed with a rational nature than in others. For only rational substances have mastery over their actions. They are free to act or not to act. The irrational substances are more passive in their actions than active. These considerations make it advisable to give the rational hypostases a name of their own, namely *person*" (*De pot.* q. 9 a. 1 ad 3). Even if the ontological aspect is treated and emphasized primarily in the Thomistic conception of person, the latter is not without its references to the psychological and the ethico-juridical meanings of person and personality.

2. *Faith and Knowledge*

Thomas is convinced that the human intellect can reach into the realms of the supersensible and behind the phenomenal world, that in its thought it can attain and understand the essence, the proper being, of things.

Nevertheless the metaphysical order does not represent the highest point of human knowledge. There is a world rising above the cosmos of metaphysical truths, the realm of the supernatural, in which God lives and reigns. This realm is not attainable here below by the mere exercise of our natural powers of mind, but rather through revelation and faith. There is question here of truths that the human mind cannot glean out of nature, not of intra-mundane truths, but of supernatural truths, revealed to us by God, which we accept with the conviction of faith, not because we understand them, but because God has revealed them to us.

The Twofold Way of the Knowledge of God. The Reality of Supernatural Truth. God is the content of a twofold knowledge, natural and supernatural. There are truths about God which lie entirely beyond the reach of human reason; e.g., the truth that there are three persons in God. But there are also truths about God which human reason can attain of its own accord, as God's existence, monotheism.

That there should be truths about God that are unattainable by the human mind when dependent entirely on its own powers, can be seen from a consideration of the peculiar nature of human thought. Our thinking is dependent on sense experience. Sense objects, as faint reflections and works of God, only tell us that a God exists, but do not reveal to us His own inner nature and life. In fact, the gradation of intellectual powers permits us to hold *a priori* that there are truths accessible to a higher mind, but not to a lower one. Thus the human mind cannot attain to all that the angelic spirit knows. The angel in turn cannot with the intellectual power peculiar to his nature attain to all that is known by the divine Intellect ever actively intuiting the divine Essence. Just as it would be folly for the peasant to consider the theories of a philosopher false merely because he does not understand them, so it is evidently foolish for man to consider the supernatural truths revealed by God as errors just because he has no full insight into these truths. The limitation of the human mind in the realm of natural truth is likewise a sign of the possibility and reality of supernatural, supra-rational truths. There are many qualities of the things about us that we do not know, and in many cases we are unable to find the deeper explanation of the qualities and phenomena which we perceive in them. How much more, then, does not the infinitely superior, divine substance, ranking infinitely above the knowable things of this world, transcend the scope of natural human reason! Thomas here refers to the Aristotelian idea, that our intellect is to the highest and first being, which is in itself most knowable, as the eye of the night bird is to the light of the sun — an idea also used by German mysticism (Henry Suso) to indicate the insufficiency of the human mind in matters of God.

We have then two ways leading to God, the way

of natural reason proceding from the works of God in nature, and the way of faith, which reaches higher, into the regions of the inner essence and life of God (*Contra gentes* I, 3).

The Natural Truths about God as Content of Supernatural Revelation. The truths about God that can be attained by natural reason are to a great extent also content of revelation and faith. This is a matter of infinite wisdom and purpose. If men were exclusively dependent on their natural abilities for attaining these truths, only few men would possess a natural knowledge of God. The majority of men would for various reasons be unable to devote themselves sufficiently to energetic thought, and to attain these truths as the fruits of their own mental labor.

Weaker mental gifts, care for family and temporal well-being, and again indolence, would prevent many from arriving at the peak of human thought. Only a few would, in the urge to knowledge which God has implanted in every soul, undertake the ascent. Besides, a knowledge of God, attained only through natural powers, would always require a long time. Profound truths demand a more practiced mental ability. The period of youth, so full of excitement and emotion, would be least given to a searching scrutiny of such profound truths. Finally a purely natural knowledge of God is always liable to error, to a distortion of the image of God. Many proofs of this are furnished in the history of pre-Christian philosophy. Hence it was well for a kind and wise Providence to include also natural truths in the sphere of revelation and faith. Thus all men may with more ease possess a knowledge of God devoid of doubt and error (*Contra gentes* I, 4).

Purpose of the Revelation of Purely Supernatural Truths. We may ask ourselves whether there was any purpose in the revelation of purely supernatural, supra-rational truths. Would not the revelation of the above-mentioned natural truths have been sufficient, and quite in harmony with the peculiar nature of man? To this we must answer that if God set a supernatural end for man, He had also to reveal to him the realm of supernatural truths.

No one strives with ardent longing for a goal unknown to him. Now man is by the providence of God called to a goal, the possession of a good, that transcends the experience of our limited mundane existence. Hence the human mind had to be directed and led to something higher, something transcending the powers of natural reason. For only thus could man direct his desires and efforts to a goal supremely above the demands and conditions of this world. Christianity holds out an eternal and supernatural good; therefore man had to be equipped with eternal and supernatural knowledge.

Furthermore, the notion of God is brought out

more clearly through the revelation of supra-rational truths. For our notion of God is the more true and adequate, the more we think of God as a being transcending the natural powers of our mind. By means of the revelation of supra-rational truths about God, this knowledge of God in us is greatly promoted and rendered more stable.

There is also an ethical advantage in the revelation of supra-rational truths in so far as pride, the father of error, is thereby suppressed. There are men who, presuming on their own genius, think they can measure the entire divine being by the scope of their minds. They think only that is true which they deem true, and that all is false which is not intelligible to them. Such vanity is put in its proper place by the revelation of supra-rational truths. Finally, the human soul attains its highest perfection in the knowledge, feeble though it be, of the most sublime truths. In this also lies the source of the purest and most enduring spiritual joy (*Contra gentes* I, 5).

The Reasonableness of Faith in Supernatural Truths. It is not through lack of thought on our part that we hold fast to the truths of revelation beyond our understanding. We are quite reasonable in so doing. Christian truth indeed transcends natural reason and contains unfathomable mysteries. But in order to lead men to the acceptance of these truths, divine Wisdom made use of wonderful means going beyond the ordinary course of things. These are in part physical, like healing of the sick, or raising from the dead, and in part psychological. The latter are miracles in the realm of the mind and consist particularly in extraordinary illuminations of the soul, by which uncultured and simple men, especially in primitive Christian times, were filled with the gifts of the Holy Spirit, and received the highest gifts of wisdom and of tongues. The convincing force of these works was in no way supported by the force of arms or by the alluring prospect of worldly pleasure. On the contrary, the greatest obstacles and difficulties had to be overcome. Indeed, the greatest miracle of all is, that in spite of the fury of tyrannical persecutions, a numberless host both of simple and of most intellectual men entered upon the Christian faith, which preaches truths beyond the understanding of man, forbids the pleasures of the flesh, and disparages all that the world esteems. Enthusiastic adherence to such a religion is the greatest of miracles. It is an evident work of divine intervention, when men turn their backs upon the visible and strive only after the invisible. This turning of the world to Christianity was not the result of a sudden accident, but the work of divine providence. Proof of this exists in the fact that this wonderful spread of Christianity was foretold by the mouths of the prophets.

The miracle of the conversion of the world to Christianity is the surest proof of the antecedent signs and miracles, which later were no longer necessary because they are seen best in their effects. It would be a miracle greater than all other miracles, if the world had been converted to a belief in such elevated truths without the aid of miracles, and to the performance of such difficult works and the hope for such high things — and that through the instrumentality of simple and uninfluential men. Even if miracles do not now occur in the same numbers as in the first centuries, God still works them in our own days through His saints for the sake of faith.

Thomas therefore proves the divine origin of revelation and Christianity from the historic miracle of the wonderful spread of the Christian faith, and thus shows the reasonableness of our faith in the data of revelation. We find these considerations mentioned in detail also by the contemporaries of Thomas, especially by Cardinal Matthew of Aquasparta, and by the Franciscan Bartholomew of Bologna recently discovered by E. Longpré, O.F.M. Thomas reinforces them by pointing to the causes of the spread of Islam. The latter owes its origin and its spread to entirely different motives. Sense pleasure is the incentive of the laws and prescriptions of the religion of Mohammed. It was spread, not by supernatural miracles, but by force of arms. Its first followers consisted, not of wise men well versed in divine and human lore, but of crude inhabitants of the desert. It can point to no prophetic announcements as proof of its claims (*Contra gentes* I, 6).

Harmony between Faith and Reason. Even if Christian truth is supra-rational, it is not irrational. There can be no human contradiction between the truths of faith and the truths of natural knowledge.

The highest principles of human thought, which are immediately evident to the human mind in its first activities, and which contain in germ all natural knowledge, are true beyond doubt. Now the truths of faith in no way contradict these highest principles or the truths derived from them. For the true can be opposed only to the false, never to another truth. Now the highest principles of human thought are true, as are also the truths of divine revelation and faith because confirmed by God. Hence a contradiction between the two is impossible. Such a contradiction would revert back upon God Himself. But God is the common source of both series of truths. Knowledge of the self-evident first principles is from God in so far as He is the author of our nature. Divine wisdom itself thinks these principles. Anything contrary to these principles is contrary to the wisdom of God, and therefore cannot come from God. Hence what we accept on the basis of divine revelation cannot be in real opposition to natural knowledge.

From this it follows that arguments raised by reason against the data of faith cannot be derived consistently from the highest, self-evident principles of thought. They have no apodictical value, but are problematic or sophistic in character. Hence the possibility of showing the weakness of such arguments (*Contra gentes* I, 7). Thomas firmly upheld the harmony between supernatural and natural truth, faith and knowledge, at a time when Averroism was spreading the doctrine of double truth in Paris. According to the latter a statement could be philosophically true and quite false from the standpoint of faith, and vice versa. In this way some persons attempted the complete separation of faith and rational knowledge. In bringing together faith and reason, philosophy and theology, Thomas accorded to profane knowledge, philosophy, a sphere of its own, as well as its own principles and method. He thereby showed himself a far-seeing pioneer in the question of the independence and self-sufficiency of philosophy among the Scholastics. "His thought, therefore," says E. Gilson writing of Thomas,[2] "does not aim at achieving as economically as possible a superficial harmony wherein the doctrines most easily reconcilable with the traditional teaching of theology may find room, but he insists that Reason should de-

[2] E. Gilson, *The Philosophy of St. Thomas Aquinas*, Eng. Trans., pp. 31-32.

velop its own content in full liberty and should set
out its demands in their utmost stringency; the value
of his philosophy lies not in the fact that it is Christian, but in the fact that it is true. . . . In this lies
the whole secret of Thomism, in this immense effort
of intellectual honesty to reconstruct philosophy on
a plan which exhibits the *de facto* accord with theology as the necessary consequence of the demands of
Reason itself, and not as the accidental result of a
mere wish for conciliation."

Reason in the Service of Faith. Conviction of the
harmony between faith and knowledge shows itself
particularly in this, that reason, philosophy, is given
a service to perform in behalf of faith and of the
science of faith, theology.

In theology we can make use of philosophy in three
ways. First, we can philosophically establish the
rational truths that form the necessary presuppo-
sitions of faith; e.g., existence of God, monotheism.
Secondly, we can use the analogies of reason in order
to render the mysteries of faith more clear. Thus
St. Augustine, for instance, attempts to bring the
dogma of the Trinity nearer to our minds by means
of many analogies taken from the realm of philosophical ideas. Thirdly, we can show that the arguments brought against the truths of faith are false,
or at least inconclusive. On this last point Thomas
gives the following suggestion for the defence of

faith against unbelief: I call your attention particularly to this, that in disputations with infidels you
do not attempt to prove the truths of faith by conclusive arguments of reason. That would detract
from the sublimity of faith. The truths of faith
transcend the natural abilities of the human mind,
indeed also of that of the angels, and are accepted by
us as revealed by God. As they derive from the
highest Truth, God Himself, they cannot be false.
What is not false, cannot be successfully attacked by
a conclusive rational argument. On the other hand,
our faith, being supra-rational, cannot be proved with
conclusive arguments of reason; but likewise it cannot in any way be overthrown by cogent rational argument, just because it is true and therefore not
against reason. The efforts of the Christian apologist
must not be directed to proving the truths of faith
philosophically, but rather to showing, by laying bare
the inconclusiveness of the objections of opponents,
that the Catholic faith is not false. (*De rationibus
fidei contra Saracenos*, etc. *Procem.*) Anselm of Canterbury had inaugurated Scholasticism proper and
had pointed to the true essence of the Scholastic
method by espousing the programme inspired by Augustine: *Credo ut intelligam* — I place myself firmly
on the platform of faith in order to penetrate further
into the content of faith by means of reason. The
ideas of Thomas regarding the function of reason in

the service of faith are nothing but a further development of this position. Thomas took up this idea of Anselm, which was transmitted and lived on in the thought of Hugo and Richard of St. Victor, Robert of Melun, Simon of Tournai, and especially William of Auxerre, and formulated it more clearly and explicitly from the standpoint of a better developed conception of faith and of knowledge. The emphatic theological idealism and spiritualism of Anselm and the Victorines was conducted into the sober channel of precise and clear concepts.

Value of Observation of Creatures for the Christian Philosophy of Life. Fully convinced of the harmony between natural and supernatural truth, Thomas is not satisfied with having reason function only in the service of faith, but warmly espouses the development of natural knowledge based on created nature. He does not share the aversion to profane study so frequently noticeable in the well-meaning but short-sighted theologians of the pre-Scholastic and early Scholastic periods. A thorough study, a profound examination of creation is for him not a hindrance to Christian views, but a powerful aid.

Contemplation of the works of God brings us to knowledge of and admiration for divine Wisdom. As the genius of the artist is revealed in his works, so is the seal of divine Wisdom impressed upon the whole of creation. Contemplation of creation fills us with wonderment at the power of God, and evokes a sentiment of reverence for God in our souls. For we must reasonably conceive the power of God, of the efficient principle of things, as incomparably greater than the greatness of creation. Contemplation of creatures inflames the human heart with love for the divine Goodness. The goodness and perfection we find scattered among creatures is completely and perfectly united in God, who is the source of all good. If the goodness, beauty, and lovableness of creatures bewitch the human mind, how much more must not God draw human hearts unto Himself, since He is the prime source and fountain of all good, in comparison with whom the types of goodness found in creatures are but miserable bubbling springs. Finally, the contemplation of creatures gives man some resemblance to the perfection of God Himself. God, in comprehending Himself, sees also all other beings. The human mind, watching in the belfry of Christian life (Weltanschauung), recognizing God and then steeping itself in the contemplation of creatures, develops in itself as it were, a likeness of the divine wisdom (*Contra gentes* II, 2). All that Thomas here says in an abstract way on the religious value of contemplating nature, the mirror of divine perfections, is found with more color and feeling in the German mystics, especially Henry Suso.

The contemplation of creatures is also helpful for

the Christian by pointing the way to a refutation of erroneous notions about God. Errors in the domain of the natural often oppose and do harm to the true knowledge of God and the truth of faith. Misapprehension of the true nature of creatures has led to their being taken for the ultimate ground of things, for God Himself, so that the existence of any supramundane, supreme being was denied. Any one who does not gauge the nature and value of creatures correctly, is easily led to erroneous views on the action and government of God in the world. Thus arose dualism — the theory of two ultimate world principles, one good and one evil — the denial of the freedom of divine creation, and the false interpretations of divine providence. It is a complete mistake to say that our notions about creatures are a matter of purest indifference as to the truths of faith, so long as we have a correct notion of God. Error in regard to creatures only too readily also leads to false views regarding God (*Contra gentes* II, 3).

Difference between the Philosophical and Theological Attitudes in Regard to Creatures. Philosophy views creatures in themselves, in their natures and activities, and arranges them into different levels according to the classes of things. Christian faith does not view creatures in themselves — e.g., fire not as fire simply — but in their relation to God, i.e., in so far as they reflect the greatness of God and are related to Him. The philosopher accordingly studies in things that which belongs to their nature; e.g., regarding fire, the fact of its rising upwards. Faith views creatures from the standpoint of God, in so far as they were created by God, are subject to Him, and are ordained unto Him. No argument against the knowledge of faith can be derived from the fact that the latter disregards many characteristics of things, such as the shape of the heavens, the nature of motion, etc. Hence the aspects under which philosophy and faith view the things of nature are quite different. Likewise are the starting points of both, the principles, different. The philosopher's arguments are based on the intramundane causes peculiar to nature and natural phenomena. The beginning of faith is God, the first, supramundane cause. The supernatural revelation of God, His glory, and His infinite power, are the principles, the guiding ideas of the theological contemplation of nature. From this it is evident that the sequence of thought, the method, is also different in the two sciences. Philosophy, metaphysics, views creatures primarily in their own proper being and by means of the principle of causality attains to a knowledge of God; it treats of creatures first and God last. In theology the opposite is true. Since theology views creatures in their relation to God, it treats of God first and descends from a con-

[95]

templation of God to creatures. It is therefore more perfect than philosophy, because it more closely resembles the manner of God's knowledge. He also knows all being outside of Himself by knowing Himself (*Contra gentes* II, 4).

CHAPTER VII

EXISTENCE AND ESSENCE OF GOD

HE notion of God is at the centre of the ideology of Thomas. Knowledge of a supramundane, personal God is the proud acme of metaphysics. Insight into the mysterious inner life of God, opened to the man of faith in the doctrine of the Trinity, is the climax of theological speculation. "God is the object of theology. . . . In this sacred science everything is contemplated from the standpoint of God (*sub ratione Dei*). The content of this science is in part God Himself, and in part other beings in so far as the latter are ordained unto God as unto their beginning and end" (*S. th.* I, q. 1, a. 7). "Almost all philosophical inquiry leads to the knowledge of God" (*Contra gentes* I, 4). The theocentric character of the thought of Thomas is the reason and the source of the peculiar genius of his writings. In its light we best understand the objectivity and dispassionateness, the limpid clarity, the modesty and moderation, the peace and truth, that breathe from his works.

Out of the rich storehouse of Thomas' theological synthesis we shall here select his exposition of the proofs of God and his notion of the divine essence.

1. *Existence of God*

Knowability of the Existence of God. Proofs. The proposition "God exists" is indeed in itself and objectively a self-evident one, since the predicate is contained in the subject. But it is subjectively, for us and for our finite minds, not a self-evident, analytic judgment. For we do not comprehend the essence of God, and therefore do not understand *a priori* that the predicate *existence* is included in the subject *God*. Hence the truth of God's existence is not known immediately and intuitively, but can and must be derived from other knowledge. It is consequently capable of and in need of demonstration. Nor can we speak of an innate idea of God, according to Thomas. The desire for happiness, with which man is naturally endowed, does not yet necessarily imply an immediate knowledge of the fact that it is God alone who can satisfy this desire. But if the striving for happiness does not imply an innate idea of God, it can nevertheless serve as a premise for a proof of God. In bringing the desire for happiness and the need of God into relation with the blissful intuition of God in the next world, Thomas seems desirous only of showing that such an intuition of

God is not impossible in itself and that there is a sort of natural basis for the highest perfection of the supernatural life. We could at most speak of an innate idea of God in the sense that our natural reason and the self-evident highest principles of thought and of being can readily lead to a knowledge of God. In all of us there has been implanted by nature something that leads to a knowledge of the existence of God (*S. th.* I, q. 2, a. 1).

Since the existence of God is therefore not an immediately self-evident, nor an innate truth, but is a truth attained only by means of conclusion from premises, a question arises regarding the nature of this demonstration. There is no question here of the Aristotelian demonstration *propter quid*. The latter establishes knowledge of a thing by means of an adequate knowledge of the cause of this thing. But there is no cause above God. Hence His existence can only be proved by a demonstration *quia* — the proof to the existence of a thing — by proceeding from the known effects about us to a first and highest cause — the way of causal thought (*S. th.* I, q. 2, a. 2).

This emphasis on the *a posteriori* nature of our knowledge shows that Thomas did not accept the so-called ontological argument of St. Anselm of Canterbury. "Here Thomas of Aquin," says Baeumker,[1] "does not feebly put together the old and the

---

[1] *Witelo*, p. 302.

new even where the old has become untenable, but decisively relinquishes the inadequate old — purely conceptual proof of God — in order to substitute for it the new, the proof from causality."

In his arguments for the existence of God Thomas has given clear expression to his conviction of the demonstrability of this existence. Especially are the arguments in the *summa* (I, q. 2, a. 3) a masterpiece of definite, conclusive, and clear argumentation. Even if he makes use of previous formulations, among them Aristotle, Augustine and Moses Maimonides, " the construction of the thought is nevertheless built up quite independently. The concise, telling formulation and the lucid synthesis are really classic." [2] We cannot refrain from giving this article, which the Dominican Thomas Pègues calls a " magnificent article, and in a certain sense the most beautiful article, richest in content, of the theological *summa*," [3] even if the precision of the original must needs suffer by translation.

" The existence of God can be proved in five ways.

" The first and clearer way is the one taken from motion. It is certain, and testified to by the senses, that something in this world is moved. But everything that is moved, is moved by something other

[2] Baeumker, *Archiv fuer Geschichte der Philosophie*, 1908, p. 132.

[3] Pègues, *Commentaire français littéral de la Somme Théologique de Saint Thomas d'Aquin*. I. Toulouse, 1907, p. 110.

than itself. For nothing is moved except in so far as it is in potency towards that to which it is moved. Now a thing moves in so far as it is in actuality. For to move (something) means precisely to lead something out of potency into actuality. And a thing can be educed from potency to actuality only by something that is itself in actuality; as the actually warm, say fire, causes the wood that is warm only potentially to become actually warm, thereby moving and effecting a change in it. But it is not possible for one and the same thing to be from one and the same standpoint at once in actuality and in mere potentiality; that can happen only from different standpoints. What is actually warm cannot at the same time be only potentially warm, it is potentially cold. It is therefore impossible that anything can be from the same standpoint both mover and moved, or that it move itself. Hence everything that is moved must be moved by another. Now if the thing moving the other is itself moved, this must be effected by still another, and this again by another. We cannot proceed *ad infinitum* in this matter, for then there would never be a first mover, and consequently never any other mover; for the second and later movers move only by reason of their having been impelled by the first mover — just as the stick can move something only by reason of being moved by the hand. It is consequently necessary to arrive at a first mover who

is moved by no other. And by this all men understand *God*.

" The second way starts from the nature of efficient cause. In our sensible world we all see an
order of efficient causes. But we never find, and it is
impossible, that anything is its own efficient cause; for
it were then existing before itself, which is impossible.
Nor is it possible to proceed *ad infinitum* in the
series of efficient causes, for in any series of efficient
causes the first is the cause of the intermediary and the
intermediary the cause of the last, no matter whether
the intermediary consists of one or more causes. Now
take away the cause and there will be no effect.
Hence, if in any series there were no first cause, there
should also be no last and no intermediary. And if in
the series we proceed *ad infinitum*, there will be no
first efficient cause, and so neither a last effect or intermediary causes — which is evidently false. Hence
it is necessary to accept a first efficient cause — and
this men call *God*.

" The third way proceeds from the possible and
the necessary, and is as follows. We see some things
in the world that could either be or not be, since things
come into being and disappear, whence it is possible
for them to be and likewise not to be. But it is impossible that everything of such a nature exist forever, since that which can also not be, at some time
is not.

" Now if all things whatsoever are capable of not being, then there was at one time nothing actual. But if that were true then neither would there be anything at present. For that which is not, begins to be only by means of something that is. In the case, then, of there being nothing actual, it would be impossible for anything to come into existence; and there would now be nothing, which is evidently false. Hence not everything that is, is merely possible; there must be a necessary being among things. But every necessary being has the ground of its necessity either from elsewhere or not. For this, it is again impossible to proceed *ad infinitum* in regard to the necessary beings that have the ground of their necessity elsewhere, just as this is impossible in regard to efficient causes, as we have just explained. Consequently we must accept something that is necessary in itself, and has not received the ground of its necessity elsewhere, being rather the cause of necessity in others. And this all call *God.*

" The fourth way is taken from the different grades we find in things. For we find in things that which is more and that which is less good, true, noble, etc. But more and less are predicated of different things, in so far as in different degrees they approach that which is most; as a thing is warmer when it is more like that which is most warm. Hence something exists that is the truest, best, noblest, and consequently also the greatest being. For what is most supremely true is also most supremely being, as is stated in the second book of *Metaphysics*. Now that which in any genus is called such-and-such a thing in the supremest degree, is also the cause of all others pertaining to that genus; just as fire, which is warmest, is the cause of all warmth, as Aristotle says in the same passage. Hence there must be something that is the cause of being, of goodness, and every perfection in all things, and this we call *God*.

" The fifth way is taken from the subjection of things to guidance. We see that many things possessing no knowledge, namely physical objects, act towards a goal; which follows from the fact that they are always or almost always active in the same way in order to attain that which is best. From this it follows that they attain their goal not by accident but purposively. But that which has no knowledge tends towards a goal only through guidance by a being that has knowledge and reason, like the arrow of the archer. Hence an intelligent being exists by whom all things of nature are directed towards their goal, and this we call *God*."

2. *The Essence of God*

Thomas strives to make clear for himself whether and how we know the essence of God and give verbal expression to this knowledge. The knowledge of the existence of a thing already includes some knowledge of its essence. Hence the knowledge of God's existence gives us a bridge over which we can proceed to a knowledge of what God is. The proofs of God's existence give us, as fruitful results, the concepts of God as first unmoved mover and therefore purest act without a shade of potentiality, as first cause of all being and therefore an *ens a se,* a being existing by and of itself, as a purely necessary and absolutely perfect being, governing the world as supreme intelligence.

Before we can give a sketch of the concept of God as it existed in the mind of Thomas, or definitely answer the question he had already asked in his youth, "What is God?" it will be necessary to mention his views on the nature, methods, and value of the knowledge of God attainable on this earth.

For deciding the manner in which we know God and can speak of Him, Thomas could fall back on some excellent preceding works, both among the Fathers (Augustine, Pseudo-Dionysius, theological writings of Boethius, John of Damascene), as well as among the Scholastics (Præpositinus, William of Auxerre, Alexander of Hales). In skilfully using and developing this ready material, Thomas strikes a middle way between an anthropomorphism that reads the conditions of creatures into God, and symbolism, according to which God ever remains, for our knowledge and our language, the absolutely unattainable, the unknowable.

For Thomas our knowledge of God is mediate, derived from the effects and the impress of God in creation. It is analogical, that is, formed by means of concepts which in their proper meaning apply to creatures and hold of God only in a higher sense based on the relation of similarity between cause and effect, God and creatures. Furthermore our knowledge of God is made up of many inadequate concepts, which try in different ways to give expression to the infinitely perfect, infinitely simple essence of God. Our ideas and expressions concerning God are formed by way of affirmation or causality, of negation and of transcendence, in so far as we affirm the real perfections found in creatures of God as of their first cause, then deny of God all the imperfections found in creatures, and think of the positive perfections attributed to God in a supereminent degree (*S. th.* I, q. 13). Although this mundane conception of God is mediate, analogical, and composite, and only imperfectly reflects God's essence and attributes, it is not false, but true. There is something in God objectively corresponding to all these inadequate ideas taken together, the absolute plenitude of divine perfection (*I Sent.* d. 2, 1, 7).

After an exposition of the nature and the manner of our knowledge of God, a question arises. In what does the metaphysical essence of God consist, that fundamental determination of the divine substance, which according to our concept distinguishes God from all creatures, and from which all the other attributes of God must derive?   Commentaries on Thomas explain his position differently.   According to one class (Capreolus, Bannez, Molina, etc.), Thomas designated God's *aseity* as the metaphysical essence; according to others (John of St. Thomas, Gonet, Billuart), it is the absolute actual knowledge; and still others (Ferre, Godoy), the absolute immateriality of God.   If we let Thomas himself speak, the metaphysical essence is simply *being*, pure reality with no admixture of potentiality: " The essence of God in none other than his being " (*De ente et essentia* c. 6).   " In God his being is his essence " (*I Sent.* d. 8, 1, 1).

Jahwe is therefore truly the proper name of God (*S. th.* I, q. 13, a. 11).   As God is simply He who is, in whom there is not the slightest possibility of not being, He is entirely distinct from all created being, which possesses a received being (i.e. imparted), being restricted into definite classes.   Creatures possess being, but are not unqualifiedly being; in comparison with the plenitude of God's being, they are rather non-being than being.

If Thomas designates the *Ipsum esse* as the metaphysical essence of God, this must not be understood as the universal abstract being, τὸ ὄν, of the Neo-platonists. John Huber, Oischinger, J. Delitzsch, d'Ercole, and others, have wrongly accused Thomas of pantheism. The *Ipsum esse*, the absolute being of God, represents a real content, concrete, personal. Universal being, on the other hand, is the product of abstraction, and as such is formally only some-thing thought by the mind, having a foundation in reality only because it is a last common element of all concepts derived from reality by analysis, and is therefore predicable of all things. Thomas himself drew a clear line between the being of God and this abstract being. If we say, he remarks, that God is being, we are in no way guilty of the erroneous view that God is abstract being. This abstract being is so constituted that it cannot exist in objective reality without addition and more definite determination, while the absolutely subsistent being of God is of such a nature that nothing whatever in the realm of actuality can be added to it (*De ente et essentia* c. 6).

The *Ipsum esse* therefore distinguishes God from created being, raises Him high above all the cate-gories of finite being, safeguards His absolute tran-scendence. This *esse subsistens*, as the most actual and the richest being, separates God infinitely from abstract being, most devoid of content. This *Ipsum esse* in God is the basic element from which all the divine attributes are derived. Just because God is unlimited and absolute being, He must unite in Himself all the perfection of being (*S. th.* I, q. 4, a. 2, and 3). If we analyze this concept of the essence of God into its historical components, we shall see Thomas as a theologian of vast synthetic powers. In his formative mind we find united and harmonized the thought of Aristotle and the speculation of Avicenna, the teaching of the Fathers (Pseudo-Dionysius, Augustine, Hilary of Poitiers, John Damascene), and the early Scholastic notions of Anselm of Canterbury, Bernard of Clairvaux, etc. Under the skilful hand of a master these various historical threads were woven into such a unified picture that only the practised eye of a master can distinguish the special coloring and character of the various historical components.

Thomas' concept of God was not a mere abstraction, offering nothing for human will or life. This we can see from the German mystics of the Dominican order, who appropriated the Thomistic concept of God and applied it in their pursuit of Christian virtue. The " *Usrithunge, was got ist und wie got ist* " of Henry Suso is nothing but Thomas' and Bonaventure's concept of God in the charming garb of mysticism.

CHAPTER VIII

GOD AND THE WORLD

*HE Divine Creative Act. The Notion of Creation.* The relation existing between God and the world is determined by the divine act of creation, by the concept of creation. Thomas, whose mind had been enriched by the creationist theism of Christianity, is clearer and goes much farther than Aristotle, who never arrived at a notion of creation despite remarkable approaches to it.

Thomas' theory of creation is under the complete dominion of his concept of God. His proof of the origin of the world by divine creation is based on this concept. It is necessary for us to accept that all beings were created by God. Whatever exists in a thing as something that has been imparted, must be caused by a principle in which that something exists essentially. Now God is essentially being. He *is* by virtue of His essence, and He alone is thus essential being. All being outside of God is imparted being. Hence all things have been produced by God. In his exposition of the relation of participated being to essential being, Thomas uses a Neoplatonic notion of the *Liber de causis*. He also believes himself to be in agreement with Plato, according to whom unity is prior to all multiplicity — this is a Pythagorean notion — and with Aristotle, who taught that the supreme being and highest truth is the cause of all being and truth (*S. th.* I, q. 44, a. 1).

According to Thomas creation means the production of a thing in its entire substance, of which there was no previous substrate that is uncreated or that was created by a non-divine principle (*S. th.* q. 65, a. 3). Hence creation is the bringing forth of substance, of being, production of being in so far as it is being (*S. th.* I, q. 44, a. 2).

Creation, as the bringing forth of being, is an act proper to God. Of all effects, the most extensive and most universal is being. Hence the latter can only be the peculiar effect of the first and most universal cause. Being as such can be produced only by God, and created causes can effect only a specific mode of being, a determination or delimitation of being, and that, in dependence on and under the sustaining hand of the first cause (*S. th.* I, q. 45, a. 5). Thomas stresses creation as the exclusive prerogative of God to such an extent that he will not admit God could allow a creature to take part in creation as instrumental cause.

Time-Character of the World. In regard to the beginning of the world, Thomas teaches that, as a work of free divine will, the world did not need to be eternal, and that it was actually not from eternity but created in time as is known from revelation (*S. th.* I, q. 46, a. 1 and 2). So much being understood, he asks the question whether the world-in-time necessarily had to be such, or, in other words, whether reason can prove apodictically that the world necessarily had to have a beginning and could not possibly have been created from all eternity. The Arabian Motacallinim, as also Bonaventure and the majority of the Scholastics, denied the possibility of an eternal creation of the world on the ground that it was self-contradictory. But Thomas taught that we know of the world's beginning in time only through revelation, and that pure reason could not prove conclusively that an eternal creation is impossible. He came to this conclusion under the influence of Moses Maimonides, and still more because of an apologetic consideration. For if we proclaim as decisive a rational argument in favor of an article of faith, which is in reality not convincing, respect for faith is thereby diminished (*S. th.* I, q. 46, a. 3).

The Divine Idea of the World. God is not only the first cause in the sense of being the efficient cause that brought forth substance and being; He is also the exemplary cause of all being. In creating substance and being, God realizes His divine ideas.

The idea is the exemplar according to which an efficient cause endowed with reason and free will produces anything. The idea is the principle of activity, and as such belongs in the realm of practical knowledge. It is also the principle of knowledge, and in this respect is likewise the point of departure of theoretical knowledge (*S. th.* I, q. 15).

We see the world as an orderly phenomenon, not as a chaos of accidental happenings. Mundane objects have definite, fixed forms. In order to bring forth anything, a prototype is necessary, so that the effect have a definite, strictly circumscribed form. Thus the artist brings his materials into definite forms on the basis of the guiding idea in his mind, an idea that either comes from the external world or lives in his mind. Now the order and definiteness of forms in the universe must be traced to a first principle, namely divine Wisdom, which thought out the order found in the variety of earthly things. Hence the prototypal forms, the ideas of all things, exist in the divine Wisdom (*S. th.* I, q. 44, a. 3).

Thomas, therefore, admitted the theory of the divine ideas into his theodicy. In this again he is the theologian of synthesis and mediation. He

agrees with Aristotle's criticism of the Platonic theory
of ideas, but accepts the theory of ideas as corrected
and developed by Augustine. In teaching the divine
exemplarism Thomas is one with the older school of
Franciscans, even if as an Aristotelian he holds back
on the question of the epistemological application of
this divine exemplarism.

Finality in the World. The universe is made up
of all created beings, as a whole is made up of its
parts. If we now examine the purpose of the whole
and of its parts, we arrive at the following position.
First of all, we see that the parts exist for their own
peculiar functions; e.g., the eye primarily for the
function of sight. Secondly, we see that the lower
parts serve the higher and more noble parts; e.g.,
the senses serve reason, and the lungs serve the heart.
Thirdly, it cannot be denied that all the parts taken
together function towards the perfection of the
whole, just as matter has its goal in form. For the
parts are, as it were, the matter of the whole. Finally, man exists because of an end outside himself,
namely the possession of God. Thus, in the entire
universe, every creature exists first of all for its own
activity and perfection. Then the lower creatures are
there for the higher and nobler. The beings inferior to man were created for man. Again, all the
individual creatures likewise function for the perfection of the entire universe. Finally, the entire

universe in all its aspects is ordained towards God
as its last goal. In all creatures the divine goodness
is reflected unto the glorification of God. In addition to this reflection of divine goodness, there is a
special manner in which God is the end of rational
creatures, since they can attain unto God by their own
activity, by knowledge and love (*S. th.* I, q. 65, a. 2).

Divine Conservation of the World. Thomas
shows the vigor of his concept of creation and the con-
sequential nature of his conception of God in his
views on the divine conservation of the world and
on the divine co-operation with the activities of
creatures. It is a truth both of faith and of reason,
that creatures are conserved in their existence by
God. Nor is this conservation merely negative or
indirect, not a mere non-destruction, but a direct,
positive conservation, which, in its continuous im-
parting of the being given in creation, is a continued
creation. The being of all creatures is dependent on
God in such a way that they would not be able to
continue to exist even a moment, and would sink back
into absolute nothing, without the sustaining activity
of the divine power.

The inner reason for this is to be found in the essence of all created being as imparted being, that of
ens ab alio (being from another). Every effect is
dependent on its cause, just in so far as the latter *is*
its cause. If a thing is only the cause of the changes

in another, the latter is dependent on the former only at the moment of changing. For instance, a house is dependent on the builder only at the time of its building. Now God is the cause not only of the becoming in creatures, but of their very being. Created being is essentially imparted being, *ens ab alio,* and that, not only at the moment of its coming into being, but also in all following moments. Hence this dependent being has need of the essential and absolute being as of the sufficient ground of its existence, not only in the first moment of its existence, but also at every subsequent instant. Every creature is related to God as the air to the illuminating sun. As the sun is essentially light, and the atmosphere becomes bright and illuminated only by participation in the light of the sun, so God alone is essentially being by virtue of His essence, simply because it is His essence to be; while creatures on the other hand are beings only by participation since their essence is not to-have-to-be (*S. th.* I, q. 104, a. 1).

Divine Concourse. For Thomas the relation of God to the world is one of transcendence, since he emphasizes the infinite contrast between God, essential being, and the creature, imparted being. Nevertheless his concept of the divine conservation of the world bridges the infinite span between God and the world and brings them into an inner and most intimate contact. This immanence of God in the

world becomes more emphatic and intimate in the
light of the Thomistic teaching on the concourse of
God with the activities of free and unfree creatures.
Thomas here strikes a middle way between the oc-
casionalistic interpretation of the action of creatures
and the deistic repression or elimination of the divine factor.

God co-operates with every act performed by a
creature. He is coactive in every created activity, and
that from the threefold aspect under which anything
can be a principle of activity: final, efficient, and
formal causality. As final cause God co-operates
with every creature in so far as its action takes place
because of a real or apparent good; and as nothing is
or can seem to be good, except through similarity
with the highest good, God. As efficient cause God
is active with every created action, because in a totality of interrelated principles of activity, the secondary agent always operates by virtue of the primary agent. For the first agent moves the second
to action. Hence all things are active by virtue of
the power of God, who is thus the cause of all the
activities of creatures. As formal cause, God is the
cause of created activities, in so far as He furnishes
the forms, the immanent principles of activity, preserves them, and applies them to action. Now the
form is immanent in the active being; and the degree
of immanence increases as the form is more funda-

mental and general. The first, most universal, and therefore most immanent form in all things is being. And since God is in the proper sense of the term the cause of this being, we see again how He is most intimately active in all things (*S. th.* I, q. 105, a. 4. Cf. *De pot.* 3, 7).

For Thomas the free actions of rational creatures are in no way outside the range of this divine causality. Nor does he see an insoluble contradiction between the sovereign universal causality of God and the self-determination of creatures. "A free will is the cause of its own action, because man by his free will moves himself to action. But it is by no means necessary to the concept of freedom that the free creature be the first cause of its own activity, just as little as a thing, to be the cause of another, must be the first cause of the latter. God is the first cause, moving both the causes that act by nature and without freedom, and those that are freely active. And just as God, in moving causes that act by necessity of their natures, in no way takes away their natural activity, so his moving influence on free causes in no way implies that their actions lose the character of freedom. On the contrary, it is precisely by his causal motion that he effects in them the character of voluntariness " (*S. th.* I, q. 83, a. 1 ad 3).

Divine Providence and Government of the World. By divine providence Thomas means the eternal plan

[118]

in the divine intellect, according to which mundane things tend to their final end. The realization in time of this eternal plan is God's government of the world.

The reality of providence is derived from the truth that God is the cause of everything good in the world. All that is good in the world is the work of God. But God creates things through His intellect. Hence there must be ever-present in the divine mind an eternal plan, an eternal picture of the good which He effects. Contemplation of the world tells us not only that things are good as substances, as individuals, but also that the tendency of things to an end, to the last end, is good. Hence the goodness of this final order must also be the work of God. And of this there must also be an eternal plan in the mind of God; that is, there must be a divine providence.

The universality of this providence follows from the universality and the efficacy of the divine causality. Since every active principle acts for an end, the direction of things to their end on the part of God — that is, the divine providence — must extend as far as the divine causality; it must, therefore, extend to whatever is in any way a being, to everything that exists in the world. Because of this universality of divine providence, it follows that there is for God no surprise, no accident, no crossing of plans, such as we experience in the activities of particular, created causes.

Through the universality of the divine providence, we can understand the existence of evil in the world. For God's providence extends to the totality of existing things, and can therefore permit a deficiency in this or that being, by which the perfection of the totality is brought about or promoted. If there were no evil in the world, much good would also never come about. The life of the lion is impossible without the death of other animals, and the heroic virtue of the martyrs would never have existed without the fury of persecution.

The freedom of the human will can be harmonized with the universal character of divine providence in like manner. For the act springing from free will as from a particular cause is an element in the universal order of all things towards God, the first cause, and is therefore also within the scope of divine providence. There is a more excellent providence reigning over the just than over the godless; from the former God holds off all that could definitely destroy their welfare. If God does not forcibly snatch the godless from their sins, this does not exclude them from His providence. For He preserves them in their existence.

Again, the universal extent of providence in no way excludes its immediacy. The divine plan embraces not only the system of created causes, but also their effects. In the execution of the divine plan, in the government of the world, God makes use of created intermediaries. He directs the lower through the higher. In this he shows the superabundance of His goodness, in so far as He imparts also to creatures the higher dignity of causal efficacy (*S. th.* I, q. 22).

CHAPTER IX

NATURE OF THE HUMAN SOUL

AN, a unified nature composed of
spirit and matter, is on the dividing
line between two worlds. For
Thomas, man is a favorite object of
philosophical and theological speculation. He devoted extensive ar-
ticles of his theological (*S. th.* I, qq. 75–90; I–II,
qq. 22–48) and his philosophical (*Contra gentes* II,
46–90) *summæ*, and of the *Quæstiones disputatæ*
etc., to psychology. The latter is considered the
masterpiece of his system, and at the same time that
part of his speculation in which he most successfully
established and justified the philosophy of Aristotle
against the contemporary counter-currents. His
philosophy of the soul is indeed chiefly metaphysical
in trend, and in this respect offers ideas of permanent
value, but an empirical basis is by no means wanting.
His theory of the emotions (*S. th.* I–II, qq. 22–44),
of memory and the exercise of memory (Commentary

on Aristotle's *De memoria et reminiscentia*), his remarks on the process and the progressive development of teaching and learning (*De verit.* 11), are very remarkable proofs of an introspective analysis of mental life.

The entire structure of his psychology is coherently and consistently built up on his conception of the essence of the soul and of its relation to the body.

The Essence of the Soul. In examining and determining the essence of the human soul, Thomas begins with the consideration that we mean by soul the first principle of the phenomena and activities of life, immanent in all living beings, whose noblest acts are self-movement and knowledge. From this consideration he is led to the conclusion that the soul cannot be corporeal. Indeed, something corporeal can be a principle of life, as the eye or the heart, but not the *first* principle, the ultimate, immanent basis of life. For, to be a principle of life and a living being is not the property of bodies in so far as they are corporeal. Else everything corporeal should have to be living and a principle of life. If a corporeal being shows manifestations of life and is in some way a principle of life, the only explanation for this can be found in that which makes this body to be just this kind of a body, namely, a living body. And this is its act (entelechy). Hence the soul, as the first principle of life in living things, is not a body, but

[123]

the act, the first actuality, of the body. Thus Thomas subscribes to the Aristotelian definition of the soul as the first actuality (entelechy), the basic act (*actus*) of a physical organism capable of life (*S. th.* I, q. 75, a. 1).

From a contemplation of the soul in general, Thomas proceeds to a more specific determination of the essence of the human soul. By human soul we mean the first immanent principle of intellectual activity. Thereupon he proves the immateriality and the substantiality of the human soul. For the former, he starts from the nature of human thought. It is a fact that man's intellect can know the natures of all things. The knowing principle can have nothing of the known objects in itself as physical determinations of its own. For that would prevent the knowledge of objects. Thus the tongue, when affected by something bitter, tastes no sweetness, but tastes all things as bitter. In the same way the intellectual principle, the human soul, could impossibly know all bodies, if it were itself of the nature of a body. For every corporeal being has a determinate nature. Were the soul corporeal by nature, or were its intellectual activities performed through corporeal organs, it would be determined and limited to such an extent that it could not possibly know the essences of all corporeal things. The unhampered range of human thought is therefore a proof that the soul, the principle and basis of this intellectual power, is incorporeal, immaterial (*S. th.* I, q. 75, a. 2). Elsewhere (*S. th.* I, q. 50, a. 1; *Contra gentes* II, a. 49) Thomas established the fundamental difference between the intellectual soul and bodies from the fact of self-consciousness, the ability of the intellect to reflect upon itself and its activities.

The immateriality of the human soul leads us to its substantiality. The subsistence of the principle of mental activities is evident from the fact that it performs a function in which the body has no share. Now that which is active by itself also exists by itself. For the manner of action corresponds to the manner of being, and vice versa (*S. th.* I, q. 75, a. 2). When we say that the mental activity is one in which the body has no share, we mean that for thinking and willing, the body is not necessary *as the organ* of mental activities. The body, however, plays a part in regard to the content of intellectual human knowledge; that is, in furnishing the materials of intellectual knowledge (*Ibid.* ad 3).

The human soul differs profoundly from the animal soul by reason of its subsistence. For according to Aristotelian doctrine thought alone of all the activities of life occurs without a corporeal organ. A soul that is exclusively the principle of sensory and not of intellectual activities — and such is the animal soul — performs no acts that are subjectively independent of matter. Hence it possesses no subsistent existence, independent of matter (*S. th.* I, q. 75, a. 3). Thomas is therefore a decided champion of the immateriality and substantiality of the human soul. For him there is no thought of an actualistic conception of the soul. By emphasizing the substantiality of the soul he rounds out the proof for its spirituality and for its fundamental difference from the animal soul. The spiritual nature of the soul is made clearer by the view that, like all spiritual substances capable of knowing general forms, the soul is not composed of matter and form. This is already evident from the soul considered in itself. For it is contained in the very concept of soul that it is the act, the first actuality, of the body. And matter, as potency, can never be a part of act. Most emphatically, however, is the absence of a composition of matter and form in the soul, as in all spiritual substances, evident from the fact that the intellect can know universal forms. Were matter part of the soul, then these forms would be known as individuals. For anything that is received in a subject, is received according to the peculiar state of this subject. The sensory powers, which make use of corporeal organs, can take up only individual forms (*S. th.* I, q. 75, a. 5).

From the spirituality and substantiality of the human soul, we can conclude to its indestructibility and immortality. The soul cannot be destroyed *per accidens;* that is, not by reason of the destruction of an other thing with which the soul is linked up. Accidents and material forms perish when the whole being is destroyed. Animal souls perish as soon as their bodies are destroyed; for they are not subsistent essences. The human soul, on the other hand, is a subsistent being, and therefore does not cease to be when something else bound up with it, the body, is destroyed.

Nor can the human soul perish *per se,* that is, by reason of its own nature. This again follows from its nature as a subsistent form. For that which *per se* belongs to a form is inseparable from it. Now existence belongs to the form *per se,* since the latter is act, first actuality. Hence matter receives its being and actuality from the fact of being united with the form; and it is destroyed by being separated from the form. Now it is impossible for a form to be separated from itself. Hence it is also impossible for a subsistent form to cease to exist. To this ontological argument a psychological one is added. There is in the human soul a natural desire to live forever. Such a natural longing cannot be vain. Hence the human soul is immortal (*S. th.* I, q. 75, a. 6).

Relation of Soul and Body. A further development of the nature of the soul is met with in the question of the relation of soul and body. It is in the concept of the relation of soul and body that we meet historically with a characteristic phase of Thomistic speculation. Through it we can get the best survey of Thomas' psychological edifice in all its orderliness and consistency. This is especially true of his theory of knowledge. Thomas has here departed from the Platonic path walked by Augustine, Hugo of St. Victor, and, to a great extent, the older Franciscan school. According to them the emphasis in defining human nature was put on the soul to the extent of ultimately making the soul the true man and considering the body merely as an organ of the soul, and not as an essential constituent of the whole man.

Over against this view, Thomas, in close adherence to Aristotle, stressed the position that the soul is not the man. For sensory perception is certainly a human activity, and at the same time not an activity purely of the soul. Hence man is not only a soul, but a composite of soul and body (*S. th.* I, q. 75, a. 4). Here Thomas strikes a middle way between spiritualism and materialism.

In order to indicate the true relation between soul and body, Thomas makes use of hylomorphism, the Aristotelian theory of matter and form. Albert the Great had already adopted this theory in a general way, and Thomas developed and systematized the view of his teacher.

It may be well to recall the basic lines of the Aris-

[128]

totelian theory of matter and form as reflected in the philosophical speculation of Thomas. Matter and form are the essential constituents of all physical objects. Everything in nature is a synthesis of matter and form. Matter is the purely undetermined, but therefore the determinable; it is the common substrate of all things of nature. It is on the dividing line between reality and nothing; it is not the really existing, but the possibility of being; it is the pure, but real, potentiality of the totality of physical nature. Therein its " entity " is exhausted.

That which makes matter to be an actual and specifically differentiated being is the form. The latter is the principle of specific being. And since the activities flow from the being, it is also the principle of activities of the thing. The form gives us the ideal factor in things. Through the form the objects of nature are reflections of the divine idea; in their forms things are knowable.

The relation of these two constituent, basic elements can be defined more precisely. Matter (potency) is passive, the principle receiving being and action; while form (act) is active, the principle giving being and action. These two opposites are harmonized in the substance of the physical thing, the composite of the two. Neither matter nor form alone constitute the essence of the physical object, but both together. Matter by itself has no existence;

it possesses reality only in union with the form. And just as it has no existence, so also matter in itself cannot be known; it is known only through the form. While matter cannot exist apart from the form, not even through the causality of God, it is possible for form to exist by itself without the support of matter; and it actually happens. Accordingly a distinction is made between subsistent and non-subsistent forms. The first are spiritual beings, pure spirits and human souls. The second are the formal principles of all irrational beings, from the animal and plant souls down. In speaking of matter and form, we have in mind " first matter " and " substantial form." From the latter we must carefully distinguish the accidental form. The substantial form, the essential form, constitutes the substance in its essential being, gives primary and specific being to it. The accidental form is, as it were, superadded to a substance already constituted in its being, and gives it secondary being.

Thomas applies the theory of Aristotelian hylomorphism to the relation between soul and body, which he expresses as follows: " The principle of intellectual activity, the rational soul, is the essential form of the human body."

This proposition is based, first of all, on the activities of intellectual life. That which constitutes the first and most basic principle of the activities of a thing is also its substantial form, the essential form of the thing, to which these activities are attributed. The reason for this is that nothing is active except in so far as it is in act. Hence everything is in action, is active, by reason of the same principle through which it is in act or possesses its primary and specific being. Thus the soul is the first and most basic principle of activity in all the levels of living beings. All activities and phenomena of vegetative, sensory, and intellectual life in man have their ultimate basis in the human soul.

Hence the principle of intellection, whether we call it intellect or intellectual soul, is the essential form of man, the form of the body.

If any one wishes to deny the force of this argument and refuses to accept the soul as the form of the body, he must furnish another explanation of how we can conceive the intellectual act as the act of man, as the function of the human self. The consciousness of each one tells him that it is his *self* which performs the act of thought. Thomas examines in their historical order the various attempts at explaining, without admitting the soul to be the essential form of the body, how the intellectual act can be that of the human self. None of these satisfies him. Only the Aristotelian theory, according to him, shows satisfactorily how it is " this individual man who performs the act of thinking." A further argument for his theory is based on the specific nature of man. The nature of a thing is manifested in its activities. Now the activity peculiar to man as man is rational thought, since therein he transcends all other living beings. Hence it is the principle of thought that determines the specific nature of man. That which specifies the nature of a thing is its essential form; and so the principle of intellectual activity in man, his rational soul, is the essential form of man (*S. th.* I, q. 76, a. 1).

Acceptance of the human soul as the essential form of the body, in no way argues against the spiritual and substantial nature of the soul. For the higher and nobler a form, the greater is its dominion over corporeal matter, the less is it also immersed in matter, and the better does it preserve activities removed from matter. The human soul, representing the highest level of substantial forms, by its own powers excels corporeal matter, in so far as it possesses a power and activity in which the corporeal matter has no part. That is its intellectual ability (*Ibid.*).

Various other considerations help to define and illumine this basic thesis of Thomas. Against the monopsychism of Averroës he shows that there are as many intellectual principles, or substantial forms, as there are human bodies (*S. th.* I, q. 76, a. 2). Again he speaks up for a single soul in the individual man, a spiritual soul. The latter, numerically one, is the principle of the intellectual, sensory, and vegetative life in the individual man; it is the one source of the intellectual and perceptual faculties, of the physical life of man (a. 3). It is at the same time the only substantial form in man. As the intellectual soul virtually contains in itself the sensory and vegetative souls, so it also virtually contains in itself all lower substantial forms, and alone performs all the functions exercised by the animal soul in the animal, and the vegetative soul in the plant (a. 4). Since the intellectual soul is the only substantial form of man, the union of body and soul is an immediate one, and is not effected by means of accidental determinations or a corporeal form (a. 6 and 7). Since the soul is the essential form of the body, it exists whole in the entire body, and whole in every part of the body. For the essential form is at the same time the perfection of the whole and of its parts. But if the soul is essentially in the entire body, this does not preclude that it develops and exercises its powers and activities in special parts, as in the brain and sensory organs (a. 8).

Thus Thomas applies the notion of the substantial form to the relation of soul and body in man in a thoroughly consistent manner, thereby bringing the essential unity of man into clear relief.

Thomas' theory, particularly his emphatic insistence on the oneness of the substantial form in man, was attacked as an innovation by the Franciscan theologians. The biographical sketch in preceding pages has already indicated that John Peckham opposed Thomas vigorously on this point. In the *Correctorium fratris Thomæ* of William de la Mare, the article in which Thomas defends the oneness of the substantial form in man is one of the principal points of attack; while the Dominicans, who wrote against William de la Mare, defended Thomas energetically just on this point. The latter is also the principal objective of the tracts *De unitate formæ* by William of Hotun, Thomas of Sutton, and especially Giles of Lessines and Hervæus Natalis. Likewise does the literature of the *Quæstiones quodlibetales* of the Dominican school treat the point thoroughly. An end was made to these attacks on the psychology of Thomas by the definition of the Council of Vienna declaring that the rational soul is the immediate essential form of the body — which definition was directed against the Franciscan Peter John Olivi. The teaching of Thomas on the relation between soul and body certainly comes closer to the text of the Council than the teaching of his opponents. The canonist John Andrea (d. 1348) refers directly to Thomas in his exposition of the text of the council: "Any one desiring further knowledge on this point, can find it in the *summa* of St. Thomas."

Thomas' doctrine of the relation of soul and body continues in the Thomistic philosophy of today. In the psychology of Cardinal Mercier, which takes full account of the results of modern research, the question of body and soul is developed in complete harmony with Thomas, and the latter is found to agree well with the assured results of experimental psychology. In fact, as the Cardinal pointed out, it is precisely in the light of this theory that we can best understand the peculiar nature of human thought.

CHAPTER X

INTELLECTUAL KNOWLEDGE OF MAN

CCORDING to Thomas the soul is a spiritual substance, immediately united with the body as its true and only essential form, and as the ultimate basis of all human, intellectual, sensory, and vegetative functions of life. The soul does not exercise these functions immediately, through its essence as such, but by means of real powers, with which it is endowed, and which are really distinct from its essence. The powers of the soul are determined and classified according to their respective acts, and these in turn according to their objects. In the last analysis, therefore, the faculties are distinguished by the formal objects of their activities (*S. th.* I, q. 77, a. 1–3).

By proclaiming a real distinction between the faculties of the soul and its substance, Thomas parts company with Augustine, William of Auvergne, and others, and adheres to Aristotle's theory of the faculties, which had been further developed by Avicenna.

[136]

Like Aristotle, Thomas accepts five basic classes of faculties: vegetative powers, powers of sense perception, the sensory appetency, spontaneous movement, and the intellectual powers (*S. th.* I, q. 78, a. 1). As far as the knowledge process is concerned, the powers of sense perception are divided into the five external and the four internal senses. The latter are the common sense, the imagination, sensory judgment (instinct), and memory (*S. th.* I, q. 78).

Just as this division adheres closely to Aristotle and Avicenna, so does the classification of the higher faculties of the soul remain faithful to the Stagirite. In fact, it is in the manner in which he analyzes the powers and activities of human thought that we can best see the Aristotelian character of the espistemology of Thomas over against the Augustinian theory of the Franciscan school. The thorough difference between the two tendencies, which we may label Aristotelianism and Augustinianism, can be indicated in the following way. Plato, Augustine, and the Franciscans, Bonaventure, Matthew of Aquasparta, John Peckham, Roger Marston, William of Falgar, etc., very decidedly stress the activity of the faculty of knowledge, the vital and subjective element in the genesis of human knowledge. Thomas and his school (Thomas of Sutton, Bernard of Trilia, John of Naples, etc.), following Aristotle, stress the passive and receptive character of knowledge, and see in knowledge an assimilation of the knowing subject with the object known, a figurative grasping of the reality.

A second point of opposition between the two is closely related to the first. In Plato, Augustine, and the Franciscans, sense perception and intellectual knowledge exist side by side rather externally and loosely. The importance of sense knowledge for intellectual knowledge is minimized. The soul, according to the Franciscans — especially Matthew of Aquasparta, their most keen-minded representative — does not acquire its knowledge of the incorporeal from the senses, but rather from reflection on itself or else in the divine ideas. Thomas, on the other hand, in close agreement with Aristotle, defends an intimate, internal relation between sensory perception and intellectual knowledge, in so far as the total content of higher knowledge is ultimately furnished through the medium of the senses. Thomas considers the manner in which man knows the corporeal intellectually as the norm and standard of human intellectual knowledge in general, therefore also of our intellectual understanding of incorporeal beings and values. Evidently this conception of the relation between sense and intellectual knowledge is an echo of the Thomistic theory of the soul as the substantial form of the body. The Franciscan school represents the predominant spiritualistic conception of human nature derived from Augustine. Let us now see how the epistemology of Thomas maintains this general characteristic in detail.

At the very beginning of his treatment of the intellectual powers, Thomas emphasizes the passive, receptive character of our intellect very decisively. He recalls the statement of Aristotle, that thinking is in a certain sense something passive, that the intellect is like an empty slate on which " nothing is written." Passivity does not here mean the purely receptive undergoing of a physical alteration, but rather the condition of being in potency to something. The human intellect is on the lowest level of spiritual beings and farthest removed from the divine intellect, the purest act, and is in potency to all intelligible things, to everything that can be an object of intellectual human knowledge. The intellect is a passive power (*S. th.* I, q. 79, a. 1 and 2).

In close conformity with Aristotle, again, according to whom there is in the soul the power to be all things and likewise to make all things, Thomas assumes an *intellectus agens*, an active intellect. The latter is a power of the human mind, which prepares intelligible (intellectually knowable) contents by means of the abstraction of the universal, the ideal, out of the materials presented through the senses. The perceptual contents of the outer world, which are brought to the portals of the intellect by the outer and inner senses, are still material and individual in character, and therefore not yet actually, but only potentially, intelligible. In order that they may become actually intelligible, that is, capable of presenting an object proportionate to the intellect's capacity for the universal and the ideal, we must assume a power in the intellect itself which can strip these materials of their corporeal and individual determinations. This active power is the active intellect. J. Mausbach brings out this function of the active intellect by a modern comparison: "It is as if X-rays fell on the sensory image and projected its immaterial form on the sensitive plate of the intellect."[1] The abstractive intellect is active, since only an active principle can lift something else out of a state of potency into actuality (*S. th.* I, q. 79, a. 3). This acceptance of an active intellect is by no means a retraction of the passivity of the intellect. For the passive intellect (*intellectus possibilis*), the intellectual faculty in which intellectual knowledge is consummated, is passive. It is receptive in regard to the intelligible forms (*species intelligibiles*) prepared by the active intellect, and by means of these is led to know. For Bonaventure, on the other hand, the abstractive intellect is not alone in being active; the passive intellect, too, is not purely passive, but endowed with a natural activity (*In II Sent.* d. 24, p. 1, a. 2, q. 4).

[1] *Grundlage and Ausbildung des Characters nach dem hl. Thomas von Aquin.* Freiburg, 1911, p. 11.

In contrast with the Averroistic interpretations and their obscuring of the Aristotelian conception of the *intellectus agens*, which is itself not too clear, and their maintaining that the active intellect is for all men a single intelligence separate and distinct from the individual human souls, Thomas declares emphatically that the intellect is in the human soul, is a faculty of the soul, whence there are as many active intellects as there are human souls (*S. th.* I, q. 75, a. 4 and 5).

In the Thomistic discussion of the intellectual faculties, that is, of the subjective factor in knowledge, emphasis is put on the passivity of knowledge. In the discussion, however, of the objects of knowledge, that is, of the objective factor in knowledge, the stress is on the intimate relation between sensory perception and intellectual knowledge, and on the decisive influence of the intellectual apprehension of the corporeal on all our intellectual knowledge in general. We have an external indication of this in the fact that Thomas begins his treatment of the objects of knowledge with the corporeal objects. In determining the manner in which sensory objects are intellectually apprehended by us, he proceeds by degrees. He first sets up the proposition that the soul, through the intellect, knows material objects in an immaterial, necessary, and universal manner. Plato removed the physical objects from the reach of intellectual knowledge because he could not harmonize the universal, necessary character of intellectual knowledge with the individual and contingent nature of sensory objects. Against him Thomas maintains both that our intellects do know the material, and that this knowledge bears the stamp of the immaterial, the universal, and the necessary. It is not necessary that the object of knowledge be received into the intellect in the ontological status it possesses in itself outside the intellect. Our intellects take up the species, the images of corporeal objects, in a manner corresponding to their immaterial nature. If even our sensory organs take up the species of gold without the actual gold, so that the gold is in the sense faculties in another manner than outside them, the intellect must all the more take up the species of the material things which are in themselves corporeal and mutable, in an immaterial and immutable form, such as is proportionate to its immaterial nature. This is expressed in the basic epistemological principle: Whatever is received, is received according to the nature of the receiver (*S. th.* I, q. 84, a. 1).

To the question of the reality of an immaterial knowledge of material objects by man, another must be added: Whether the essence of the soul in itself is the sufficient medium of this knowledge. Here Thomas sets up a proposition that illumines his entire epistemology: God alone knows everything by means of His essence, since He alone, as the first cause, has the ideas of all things in Himself. No created spiritual substance, not even an angel, knows things by means of its own essence. In man the soul as such is a medium of knowledge neither for material nor for immaterial objects (*S. th.* I, q. 84, a. 2). Furthermore, the soul does not know the material or the immaterial by means of innate ideas. This is contradicted by the potential character of our lower and higher faculties of knowledge, as experience reveals them to us (a. 3). Thomas likewise rejects the Neoplatonic theory that our souls receive the intelligible species of material objects, in fact of all objects, from other intelligences; for in that way we cannot explain the purpose of the union of body and soul (a. 4).

Another question is whether we know material objects, and *a fortiori* the immaterial, in the *rationes æternæ*, that is, in the eternal ideas of God. Thomas here takes the opportunity to explain his position over against the Augustinian-Franciscan conception of knowledge. The Franciscan school (Bonaventure, Matthew of Aquasparta, John Peckham, Roger Marston, William of Falgar, Fr. Eustachius, Walter of Bruges, etc., with whom we must associate Gerard of Abbeville and Henry of Ghent), pointing to Augustine, base the certainty of human knowledge on a contact between the human intellect and the light of supreme truth. The eternal light of the divine ideas moves our intellects and sheds a ray of light into them, so that in, and by the influence of, this light we formally know the truth. Thomas accepts the concept of a knowledge in the eternal ideas, but interprets it in the light of his Aristotelian epistemology. He rejects the view that man here below knows everything in the divine ideas as in a known object, in a medium of knowledge; he says we know all things in the divine ideas as in the first principle of knowledge only in so far as the light of reason in us is a participation in the divine light, and in so far as things, being fashioned after the divine ideas, are true and knowable (*S. th.* I, q. 84, a. 5). There can be no question here of an actual agreement between the Augustinian-Franciscan and the Thomistic conceptions of a knowledge in the divine ideas. External facts also indicate the contrary. John Peckham brings up just the theory of the *regulæ æternæ* as a point of difference between the Franciscan school and Thomas. Roger Marston expressly combats Thomas' exposition of Augustine. The Franciscans believed that Thomas interpreted Augustine differently from them in this matter and that he depreciated the latter.

The mind of man, therefore, draws its knowledge of material as well as immaterial objects neither out of the depths of its own spiritual being, nor out of the light of the divine ideas. Whence, then, does our mind derive the plenitude of its knowledge? Thomas answers that the contents of our knowledge are derived from experience. He consciously and decisively takes up the position of Aristotle, and employs the latter's dictum: "Our knowledge starts in the senses." The truth of this statement he rests on the fact that the images, which the active intellect by its abstractive power raised to ideational and intelligible species or forms, are as to content derived from the world of sense. Consequently our intellectual knowledge is dependent on sensory experience for its materials. But as the images acquire their intelligible character only through the functioning of the active intellect, we cannot call sense knowledge the exclusive and total cause of our intellectual knowledge. Sense experience is the cause of our intellectual knowledge only materially, in regard to content (*S. th.* I, q. 84, a. 6). These explanations of Thomas mark a notable difference between his own theory and that of the Franciscans. According to the latter our knowledge of immaterial objects is not derived from the senses, but arises either out of a contemplation of the soul itself or out of the divine ideas; intellectual knowledge of the material world, on the other hand, is attained through the senses.

Thomas rigorously develops the consequences of

his thesis, that the senses are the original sources of all our intellectual knowledge. He considers it impossible for our intellect, in union with the body here on earth, to perform any act of knowledge without recourse to images. He refers to experience in substantiation of this claim. Injury to a corporeal organ, which affects the imagination, also causes disturbances in intellectual life — a proof that the latter presupposes the former. Experience furthermore shows that, in order to grasp something intellectual, we employ corresponding images, analogies, etc. We do the same when we try to explain difficult matter to others. We give them examples, comparisons, which evoke the corresponding images and thereby initiate and call up a spiritual understanding of the point in question. The deeper metaphysical basis for this relation between the activities of higher thought and of imagination lies in the proportionality between the knowing subject and the known object. The proper object of the human intellect, which forms one nature with the body, is the essense of corporeal things (*quiditas in materia corporali existens*). In the realm of actual existence the specific object of human knowledge is always individual. There is outside the mind no universal nature of stone, only this or that definite stone. Hence the essence of corporeal things can be known intellectually only after the concrete material individual things are known. Now it is precisely the part of the senses and the imagination to know the individual things. The intellect must therefore, turn to the images in order to know its proper object, namely the essence inherent in individual things, the common nature existing in individuals (*S. th.* I, q. 84, a. 7).

This turning of the intellect to the images is necessary not only for our intellectual knowledge of material objects, but for our intellectual knowledge of any objects whatsoever. For we can think of incorporeal objects, of which no images exist, only by analogy and by aid of the corporeal of which we have images (*S. th.* I, q. 84, a. 7 ad 3). Pure spiritual substances think of the material after the manner and the analogy of the immaterial; we, on the other hand, think of the immaterial after the manner and the analogy of the material (*S. th.* I, q. 85, a. 1). As long as we live here on earth, neither our active intellect nor our passive intellect can enable us to know pure spirits in themselves (*S. th.* I, q. 88, a. 1).

A brief sketch must also be given of the Thomistic conception of the intellectual knowledge of individual things and of the self-knowledge of the soul. Here, again, Thomas departs from the Franciscan school. Thomas teaches that the individual material things as such cannot be the immediate and first object of our intellectual knowledge. The reason for this is that material objects are individuated by their matter.

Now our intellect knows just by abstracting the intelligible species from this matter. That which is thus abstracted, however, is universal. Hence our intellect can know only universals directly. But it can recognize individuals indirectly, and by a sort of reflection, since they can become the objects of knowledge by means of the intelligible forms only when the intellect turns to the images (*S. th.* I, q. 86, a. 1).

This theory aroused the criticism of the Franciscan school. Matthew of Aquasparta, for instance, teaches expressly that our intellect can know the individual thing directly, by means of singular species. He attacks Thomas, whose teaching he cites literally without mentioning a name, calling it difficult to understand.

Thomas solves the question of the self-knowledge of the soul in full accord with Aristotle. Our intellect knows itself in the same way in which it knows all other things. It does not know itself by means of its essence, but by means of its acts. The reason for this is the passive, potential character of our mind. For a thing *is* only in the degree in which it is act. Our eyes do not see that which is only possibly a color, but that which is actually colored. Thus also our intellect. It can know material things only in so far as they are actual being. Prime matter, for example, can be known only in its relation to substantial form. Our intellect is potential, is *intel-*

lectus possibilis. In itself it has the ability to know things; but it can itself be known only in so far as it is in act. As every act of the intellect takes place only by a turning to images, the intellect can know itself only when it is set in action by the intelligible forms abstracted out of the images by the active intellect. Hence our intellect knows itself through its acts and not through its essence (*S. th.* I, q. 87, a. 1). In this we can see the consistency with which Thomas develops his conceptions of the potential, passive character of our intellect, and of the origin of intellectual knowledge in the senses — both knit closely into a solidary epistemological synthesis. The Franciscan school rejected the Thomistic explanation of self-consciousness. Matthew of Aquasparta combated Thomas also on this point, citing the latter's views word for word. He defends the theory that the mind knows itself, its inner being, not by means of its acts, by way of logical conclusion, but directly through itself, by way of intuition.

CHAPTER XI

SYSTEM OF ETHICS

THE moral speculations of Thomas form a gigantic achievement that is also lauded by non-Catholics (among others, by Gass). The ethics of Thomas, forming the second and greatest part of the theological *summa*, and carefully treated also in other works, is highly important from the standpoint of an analysis of sources, of its systematic synthesis, and of the actual value of its contents.

Thomas made an abundant and skilfull use of the Nicomachean ethics of Aristotle. He became familiar with its contents while writing his commentary on it, for which he used the direct translation of his confrere, William of Moerbeke. Earlier Scholastics, William of Auxerre in his *Summa aurea* [1] being the first, had drawn upon parts of the ethics of the Stagi-

---

[1] *Golden Summa* — a work used extensively by Alexander of Hales and subsequent Scholastics; a summary exposition of theology, of high importance for the history of dogma.

rite. But no theologian before Thomas used the contents and terminology of this book so extensively for the formulation, foundation, and investigation of the Christian moral synthesis. It would, however, not be true to fact to consider the work of Thomas nothing but a repetition of Aristotelian ideas. Thomas intended to write a Christian, supernatural, and not a purely philosophical ethics, and therefore also drew extensively upon biblico-patristic moral speculation, especially as the latter was developed and formulated by Augustine with the aid of Stoic ideas. The moral speculations of the earlier Scholastics, especially as contained in the *Sentences* and *summæ*, particularly the *Summæ de virtutibus et vitiis* (Peter Cantor, Robert of Courçon, John de la Rochele, etc.) exerted their influence on Thomas. In an unpublished, systematic ethics of his teacher Albert the Great (*De bono*) he had a prototype of a well organized moral philosophy. In the moral theology of Thomas the mystic writings of Richard of St. Victor in particular also find their echo. Finally the *Secunda* also shows a considerable amount of canonical and liturgical knowledge.

This great variety of source materials made considerable demands on Thomas' powers of systematization. While the earlier Scholastics in general, particularly after the example of Peter the Lombard, worked out their moral problems rather

on occasions furnished by their dogmatic speculations, Thomas created a complete unified system
of morals in the second part of his *summa*. " No-
where," writes Baumgartner, " is his power of
synthesis so resplendently evident as in the field
of ethics." [2]

All morality is conceived by Thomas as the movement of rational creatures towards God (*motus ra-
tionalis creaturæ ad Deum*). In the *Prima secundæ*
(first section of the second part of the *Summa theologica*) this movement is treated in general; in the
Secunda secundæ (second section of the second part)
the particular phases of this movement are treated.
At the beginning of his general treatment we find
the goal of this movement: happiness, which is the
final end of creatures (*S. th.* I–II, qq. 1–5). This
happiness, the final end of man, is essentially and
basically the immediate vision of God in the next
world. It constitutes the highest exercise of the
highest human faculty, the intellect, in regard to the
supremest object, God, Himself pure intelligence.
From this immediate and unveiled vision of God
follows secondarily an unspeakable love and joy on
the part of the human will. While Thomas thus interprets the final end in an intellectual direction,
Scotus, in opposition to him, gives the primacy to the

[2] M. Baumgartner, *Thomas von Aquin* in: E. von Aster, *Grosse
Denker I*. Leipzig, 1911, p. 311.

will and sees the happiness of the will as the primary and essential element of our ultimate end.

The means leading to this end are the moral actions of man (*actus humani*). A good part of the general ethics (*S. th.* I–II, qq. 6–48) is given over to a psychological analysis of these acts. Especially is the role of the will in moral actions properly defined, and an acute psychological description of the various forms and steps of voluntary action given. The freedom of the will, the backbone of morality, is especially emphasized. The root of freedom of choice is reason, which presents objects of desire and motives of action to the will. The idea of the good necessarily attracts the will; the human will always acts under the aspect of the good. But while the *bonum universale*, the general aspect of happiness, naturally impels our wills, man is free with respect to individual objects of choice. He can choose or not, choose this or that. The different levels of value do not force the will; the latter decides for itself, determines itself, moves itself towards an object.

To the treatment of voluntary processes as such, of freedom of will as the objective presupposition of moral actions, is added a treatment of human acts in their objective nature, in their character of moral goodness or badness. Every action is good in so far as it participates in being, as it possesses the perfection required of it; while deficiency in its being, in the

[153]

perfection it should have, constitutes moral evil. The presence or absence of this due being or perfection is more closely determined by the object, the circumstances, and the end of the action, which are therefore determinants of moral good and evil. The aspect of end, finally, leads the goodness of human volition and action back to a harmony with the divine will, the cause of all created good. In this conception of the moral good, ethics and metaphysics come into intimate contact.

Reason and will are the chief sources of moral action. But besides them, the emotional life plays an important role in the sphere of morality. For man is a synthesis of soul and body; and as sense experience is of the greatest importance, even indispensable, for intellectual knowledge, so the ups and downs of our emotional nature are of immense influence in our moral life and endeavors. It is our emotional life that shows the intimate contact between our intellectual and our sensory natures, the interrelation between the higher and lower phases of our human nature — the echo of intellectual representations in sensory strivings as well as the conative and inhibiting influences of our passions on human will. Thomas well understood the importance of the emotions in ethics, and devoted twenty-seven questions of his theological *summa* to this topic (*S. th.* I–II, qq. 22–48). This treatise " On the Passions " contains the results of careful psychological observation. "Here," says Morgott, "we learn to know the experienced saint and mystic, who took note of the slightest stirrings of the human heart, and could detect the finest whisperings of the soul's harp, and who — more difficult still — found words and ideas for the seemingly inexpressible and rendered it accessible to human understanding." [3]

Moral acts, which receive their human coloring from their emotional character, presuppose internal and external principles. The inner principles are the natural and supernatural habits of virtue which equip the soul's energies for their tendency towards the last end, and keep them directed to it. Thomas made extensive use of the Aristotelian views on habits, and applied them to the Christian teaching on virtues and grace (S. th. I–II, qq. 49–70). The contrary of good habits is furnished by sin, which leads man away from his last end (S. th. I–II, qq. 71–89).

The external principle of moral action, which is outside and above man, is God; and that, in a twofold manner. In His law He gives us the norm, direction, content, and sanction of moral action (S. th. I–II, qq. 90–108); and then He moves, elevates, and supports us through His grace (S. th. I–II, qq.

[3] Morgott, *Die Theorie der Gefuehle im System des Hl. Thomas.* Eichstaett 1860, p. 5.

109–114). The directive and obligatory influence of divine law — here Thomas follows Augustine — traces back to the *lex æterna*, to the great plan of the world rooted in God's holiness and wisdom. All laws are derived from this eternal idea of the divine government of the world, which has the character of law. Both rational and irrational creatures are subject to it. Irrational creatures take part in the eternal law by naturally and unconsciously following the innate impulses and mechanical laws of their being, whereby they are incorporated into the general purpose of creation. In man, however, because of his rational free will, the eternal law is fulfilled with knowledge of his end and in free and conscious pursuit of it. This impress of the eternal law in the mind of man, the law written in the heart of man, is called the natural moral law. It is promulgated in him with the development of reason. Man easily recognizes the first principles of moral action, which are reducible to the proposition: Do good, avoid evil. The intellect's ready ability to recognize the basic moral principles is called synteresis by Thomas and the other Scholastics, sometimes also spark of the soul, *scintilla animæ*, a term that found favor among the German mystics of the fourteenth century. These highest principles of moral conduct are for practical reason, which judges in moral questions, what the supreme, indemonstrable, self-evident laws of being and thought are for theoretical reason. Synteresis develops into conscience, which applies the moral principles to the individual actions. In this manner God is through the natural law the external principle of morality. His legislative activity is further extended and developed in the positive relation of the Old and New Testaments, which presents us with supernatural ends, values, and motives.

If God is, through the natural and the positive-supernatural law, the external normative principle of moral conduct, He is, as dispenser of grace, the moving, assisting, and elevating principle, which comes to man from without, but enters into the intimacy of his soul. God implants a system of supernatural energies in the soul, by which the latter is elevated to an existence and activity conformable to God, and ultimately to an immediate contemplation of God.

On this general background of morality contained in the *Prima secundæ*, the *Secunda secundæ* paints the picture of a Christian life of virtue. It deals with two grand themes: the virtues themselves in their various ramifications and effects, and the different stations and forms of Christian life. With a skilfull hand Thomas groups the Christian efforts for a virtuous life about the three divine virtues, and the four cardinal virtues. In the centre of this group, as queen of the virtues, is charity, the supernatural love of God and neighbor. The presentation of the Christian life of virtue, especially the teaching on charity (*S. th.* II–II, qq. 23 ff.), and on prayer (*ibid.* q. 82 and 83), is full of warmth and feeling, and indicates a practical acquaintance with Christian asceticism and mysticism. Important in his teaching on the different stations and walks of life is his theory of the religious life, which he was the first to incorporate into theology. He does not assign to the religious state a higher form of Christian perfection, such as would disrupt the unity of the Christian ideal, which for him consists in the love of God. In his judgment of the merits of the religious life, the emphasis is on the internal disposition and on self-oblation. The evangelical counsels and the practices of monastic life are important as instruments of Christian perfection in so far as they are special means and special opportunity for a free and unhampered devotion to the life of grace and love (*S. th.* II–II, qq. 186–189).

This rapid sketch of the Thomistic moral theory, which gives us a mere glimpse of the rich content of the second part of the theological *summa*, shows us the architectonic talent, the systematizing genius of Thomas. But it also indicates the practical values we can hope to find in his exposition of moral life.

Thomistic ethics stresses the subjective and the objective, each in due measure. The moral action is said to spring out of the inner nature of man, bearing the stamp of his sensory-intellectual free nature. But this action is destined for an end high above man himself, and is therefore teleologically regulated by norms and laws that are likewise above the free choice of man, that are, consequently, reflections of a metaphysical order. Finally all moral action and life is rooted in God, just as our knowledge of truth has its deepest and last basis in God. Thomistic ethics is theocentric, but without surrendering the genuinely human, psychological side of conduct.

In the moral speculation of Thomas happiness and morality are harmonized. Even if the hope of happiness is a strong urge in striving for virtue, his is no utilitarian eudæmonism. For happiness, as he conceives it as final end, is at the same time the highest development of morality.

In Thomas a speculative bent and an empirical sense for realities work together. The method of observation, especially the careful scrutiny and analysis of the processes of the soul, plays an important part. General moral considerations, he says, are less useful than special investigations, since human actions are individual and concrete (*Prologus in S. th.* II–II). Experience is not infrequently emphasized by him as an excellent way towards the derivation of general moral principles.

Finally the ethics of Thomas is a harmonious syn-

[159]

thesis of the natural and the supernatural. Thomas was an adept at discovering the points of contact offered by nature for the supernatural, and at showing how the supernatural adapts itself so admirably to the laws and needs of the human soul. With fitting skill he draws his parallel between the organism of the seven sacraments and the stages of the development in natural human life. He never wrote an autobiography, or confessions like Augustine. But in his ethics he unwittingly gives us an insight into his rich and unified soul-life, bent on seeking God. His ethics contains not only ancient and Christian wisdom, not only the results of his own speculative efforts; it also bears the stamp of his own inner experiences. He tried to realize in his own person the ideal of the Christian life, and for that reason he could depict the beauty and grandeur of Catholic ethics so truly and clearly, so simply and impressively.

CHAPTER XII

POLITICAL AND SOCIAL PHILOSOPHY

HERE is no part of the teaching of Thomas that has attracted the attention also of non-Catholic thinkers to such an extent as his political and social philosophy. It is now known that his theory of state is no pure apriorism, but reveals a close contact with human life based on concrete materials and facts drawn from observation. His presentation of it is both clear and practical, making its appeal to sane human reason. Modern thinkers have acknowledged that many ideas of social, political, and juridical philosophy, which have been celebrated as attainments of our own times, are to be found in the writings of Thomas. Ihering, for instance, says in the second edition of his work *Der Zweck im Recht:* [1] " This great mind (Thomas) correctly understood the realistic-practical and the social factors of moral life, as well as the historical. . . In amazement I ask

[1] Ihering, *Der Zweck im Recht*, II, p. 161 f.

myself how it is possible that such truths, once they were uttered, could be forgotten so completely by our Protestant savants? What false roads would have been spared, had they taken them to heart! For my part, I should probably not have written my book, had I known them; for the basic ideas I occupied myself with are to be found in that gigantic thinker in perfect clearness and in most pregnant formulation."

From the standpoint of historical examination this part of Thomistic thought is noteworthy, because in it the Augustinian conception of state of pre-Thomistic theology is for the first time united with Aristotelian theories of state and society. It is a new synthesis in which many one-sided notions of the earlier teachings were excluded and full consideration was given to the natural needs of life and to the purposes of the individual as well as of society. " No one has had such an influence on the acceptance of Aristotle's social philosophy as Thomas. The comprehension and the independent mastery of this doctrine are his own personal merit." [2]

We first meet with Thomas' social and political philosophy in the form of an exposition and evaluation of Aristotle, namely, in the commentary on the latter's *Politics*, which had been translated into Latin

[2] Baeumker, " *Die europaeische Philosophie des Mittelalters* " (*Kultur der Gegenwart*, I, 5 ed.), p. 403.

by William of Moerbeke. Thomas develops his own
views independently in many parts of his systematic
masterpieces, especially in the theological *summa* but
also in various *opuscula* or monographs. Besides the
De regimine Judæorum ad ducissam Brabantiæ, the
De regimine principum ad regem Cypri, a political
treatise in the form of an instruction to a prince, is
important here, despite the fact that it is only partly
from the pen of Thomas himself. This treatise,
completed by Bartholomew of Lucca, led to similar
works by others. We shall only recall the *De
regimine principum* of Giles of Rome. Nor is it
mere accident that the exhortations of King Louis
the Saint to his son Philip re-echo the ideas of this
monograph of Thomas.

Because of the present value and the historical
significance of his social and political theories, it is
in place to present his main views verbatim, on the
origin, nature, purpose, and forms of civil power.

Thomas derives the origin of the state and of civil
power from the nature of man: "Wherever men
strive after a goal and can proceed in various ways,
a directing mind is needed to' show the right way to
the goal. . . Man has an end to which his whole
life and activity are directed. For he is a creature
acting through reason. For him it is therefore proper
to act for a purpose. Now it is a fact that men strive
after their end in different ways, as we can see from

[163]

the differences in human endeavors and actions. For that reason man has need of what will guide him to his end. He has indeed received the light of reason from nature, and should be guided to his end by means of it. And if man lived in total isolation, as so many animals do, he would not have need of any other directing factor. Each man would then be his own king, and under God the highest king, in so far as he would guide himself by means of the light of reason he received from God. It is, however, a demand of man's nature that he incline to life in society and state (*animal sociale et politicum*), that he live in social fellowship with many others. This is a greater natural need in man than in any other living beings. Nature supplies the animals with food, a protective dress of fur, and means of defence against enemies, like teeth, horns, nails or fleetness of foot. Man was not equipped by nature with any of these, but he received reason instead, so that with its aid his hands might procure all these things for him. But the individual man would never be able to do that, if dependent solely on himself — hence the natural need of living in fellowship with others. A similar conclusion results from the fact that animals have a much more highly developed instinct than man has for all that is useful or harmful in life. . . The latter again must supply the deficiency by means of his reason, which is only possible for him if he lives together with others. In a social fellowship one man helps the other, and various persons help by the invention of various means. One devotes himself to medicine, another to something else, etc. The clearest indication of the social nature of man is his power of speech, the ability to express his ideas clearly to others, while the animals can express their feelings only in a very general way. . .

" If, then, it is natural for man to live in society, there must also be some way in which the many are governed. In a large body of men, with the egoistic interest of each one to work for his private benefit, human society would be disrupted, unless there were some one who had care of the general good of the society, just as the body of man and of every other living organism would be dissolved if there were no common energies guiding the body, and directing all to the common good of all the members. . . There is a deeper rational ground for this.

" The individual or the personal, and the common are not the same. In the personal we have the element of distinction and separation, in the common the basis of unity and harmony. Now whatever things are distinct and different must have different causes. Hence there must be over and above the tendency of each one towards his own good, something that works towards the general good common to many. We see a guiding principle wherever many things tend towards one end. In the corporeal world the highest celestial body guides the other bodies in accordance with the orderly plan of divine providence. Again all bodies are governed by the rational creature. As in the macrocosm, so in the microcosm. In the individual man the soul governs the body, and among the faculties of the soul the irascible and concupiscible are guided by reason. Among the members of the body there is likewise one that is the most noble, is guide of the others, namely the heart or the head. In every manifold there must be a governing principle " (*De regimine principum* I, 1). Thus the very nature of man points out the formation, justification, and need of the social authority which we meet at various levels in the father of the family, the head of a community, and in its highest and truest sense in the ruler, the king of the land.

This derivation of civil authority, psychological and ethical in character, is essentially Aristotelian and receives its metaphysical support from the Platonic idea that unity must precede multiplicity. With this view we can readily harmonize the theological explanation of civil power which Thomas gathers from the Scriptures and which holds that civil authority is, like the spiritual, instituted by God. God is the creator of human nature; and since society and state are demands of nature, He is likewise institutor and source of civil authority. For Thomas the state is not merely a necessity consequent upon the first sin of man. He holds expressly that there would have been a state and society, a dominion over free men (*dominium politicum*), also in the state of innocence, that is, even if man had not fallen. There are two reasons for this. The first is the social nature of man, in accordance with which men would have lived in society even in the state of innocence; and such a societal life is not possible without an authority that is intent upon the common weal. A second reason is, that it would have been without purpose to have a situation in which men, far surpassing others in knowledge and justice, would not have been able to use their gifts for the benefits of others as rulers (*S. th.* I, q. 96, a. 4).

Types of Civil Authority. The Best Form of Government. Following Aristotle Thomas distinguishes between a good and just government, and a bad, unjust one. The former has three types: the polity (democracy, in the modern good sense), aristocracy (*optimates*), and monarchy — the distinguishing factor being whether the government is in the good hands of many, of a few, or of one. In a similar way unjust government divides into tyranny, oligarchy, and democracy (demagogy), that is, the unjust government of one man, of several, or of the people (rabble) (Cf. *De regimine principum* I, 1). For Thomas the best form of government is the monarchical. There is a greater advantage in having government over the many in the hands of one man, because in this way peace is most secure. It is also the best form because the most natural, and nature always does what is best. All directivity in nature proceeds from unity; in the multitude of members of our body there is one that moves the others, the heart; and in the life of the soul one faculty rules the others, reason. Bees have a royal ruler and in the entire universe there is one God, creator and ruler of all (*Ibid.* I, 2).

As monarchy, the just rule of one man, is the best form of government, so tyranny, the unjust rule of one, is the worst (I, 3). In order to forestall tyranny, Thomas advises a " mixed " form, in which besides the monarchical principle, that of the aristocratic form and the democratic are to enter into the constitution of the state (*S. th.* I–II, q. 105, a. 1). If a monarchy has developed into a tyranny, patience must be exercised, for the sake of avoiding greater evil. If the tyranny becomes unbearable, the people, as far as it is practicable, may proceed to action, especially in case of an elective monarchy. Tyrannicide, however, is never permissible (I, 6). In the expressions and ideas of Thomas there is no justification for the statement first made by the Parisian theologian, Jean Petit (1407), and often repeated, that Thomas taught or favored tyrannicide. Thomas paints a dark and deterring picture of the person of the tyrant (I, 3–6, 10); but he is equally vigorous in picturing the glorious character of a good king. No perishable earthly goods, neither honor nor fame, are his incentives for action and rule (I, 7); his chief motive is the reward he is to expect from God, eternal happiness, God himself (I, 8). The reward of the good king is the highest degree of happiness in heaven (I, 9). As an earthly reward he will reap the love and gratitude of his subjects (I, 10). Moreover, temporal goods, riches, power, and fame, will accrue to the just ruler rather than to the tyrant (I, 11). Thomas gives us the most ideal picture of the manner of government and of the ruling qualities of the good king. The king must be in his kingdom what the soul is in the body and God is in the world. The rule of the good and just king must reflect the divine government of the world (I, 12–14).

The Mission of the State. State and Church. To rule means to lead that which is being ruled to its proper end in a fitting manner. The mission of the state is to lead the citizens to a happy and virtuous life. If life in general were the sole end of civic society, then animals and slaves would also be parts of a political fellowship. If riches were the aim of the state, then the merchants together would consti-

tute a state. Hence the immediate mission of the
state and of its authority is that of leading the citizens to a truly good life, that is, a virtuous one (*De
regimine principum* I, 14).

In order to attain this end, the king, as the possessor of the civic authority, must use several means,
must realize, as it were, various secondary ends.
Above all, he must see that peace is firmly established
in the civic community. In his emphasis on peace as
the chief aim of the state, Thomas follows Augustine.
A second duty of the state, for the attainment of a
happy and virtuous life among its citizens, is the
fostering of favorable economic conditions, of an external prosperity (*De regimine principum* I, 15).
For the attainment of this end, Thomas stresses ag-
riculture (*Ibid.* II, 3), but without depreciating trade
and commerce. The basis of economic weal is private
ownership. A. Ritschl, Gottschik, Wendt, J. Werner,
etc., attributed a communistic theory of ownership to
Thomas. G. v. Hertling, F. Walter, F. Schaub, and
Deploige, on the contrary, came to his defence, and
have shown conclusively the difference between the
theory of Thomas and that of communism.

While the immediate, proper, and general mission
of the state is the virtuous life of its citizens, and the
special ends are the preservation of peace and the
promotion of material welfare, we have not yet
reached the highest and last end of man. There is

an end outside and above man, given him by God —
the possession of God in eternal happiness in heaven.
This is the divinely willed end of man and of society.
Hence civic society must conform itself to this higher
order of things. The highest and last end of the state
is, therefore, not only the virtuous life of the individuals, but ultimately the attainment of God. If
this end were attainable by the purely natural powers
of man, it would be the task of the king to lead man
to this final end. But the eternal union of man with
God in heaven cannot be attained by mere human
endeavors; it can be had only with the aid of God.
Hence it is not the task of human authority, but of
divine, to lead men to this end. Now the possessor
of this divine power is not a mere man, but also
God, namely Jesus Christ, who made men children
of God and opened eternal glory to them. To Him
a kingdom was given that shall never be destroyed.
He is therefore called king in Holy Writ; and not
only priest. From Him is derived a royal priest-
hood. The government of this kingdom He in-
trusted, not to earthly kings, but to priests, and first
of all to the supreme pontiff, the successor of Peter
and the representative of Christ, the Bishop of Rome
— so that the distinction between the worldly and the
spiritual realms be thus kept in mind. To the Bishop
of Rome kings of the earth must be subject as to
Christ himself. For those who have charge of the

aims and ends preparatory to the highest end must be subject to and guided by him who has care of the highest end. Authority is the nobler, the higher its end. He who represents the highest end is ever above those who are concerned for the partial ends leading up to the highest (*De regimine principum* I, 14).

Thomas thus teaches subordination of the earthly authority to the spiritual, of the state to the Church. But since this relation is guided by that of the different ends, he cannot be called a sponsor of the *potestas directa* upheld by Augustinus Triumphus and others, of an absolute power of the Pope in both temporals and spirituals. Thomas taught only an indirect power of the Church in matters temporal, according to which the Church has a word to say in temporals only in so far as these are related to the supernatural. — The Thomistic theory was thus expounded by the best commentators, Conrad Koellin, Francis of Vittoria, e. a.

CHAPTER XIII

THOUGHTS ON CHRISTIANITY AND THE CHURCH

VEN if Thomas nowhere wrote a special treatise on the Church and never gave an independent exposition of his conception of the Church, we may nevertheless obtain a practical and sympathetic synthesis of his ideas on Christianity and the Church by collating his various occasional utterances. It is particularly the dogmatic and ethico-mystic trends that give charm and beauty to his picture. His conception of Christianity and the Church bears a Pauline and Augustinian stamp, and is based on a speculative penetration of the Pauline conception of Christ as the head of the Church. The intimate and real presentation of the relation between Christ and the Church also shows the influence of Greek patristics, of St. John Chrysostom and St. Cyril of Alexandria.

The guiding basis of the Thomistic conception of the Church is dogmatic in character. It is the dogmatic conception of the inner essence of Christianity, as developed in the treatise *De lege evangelica* (*S.*

[173]

th. I–II, qq. 106–108) under the inspiration of St. Paul and St. Augustine. The primary basic force in the Church, its entelechy, is the grace of the Holy Ghost. Everything in Christianity is either an expression or effect of this interior grace or a means, a direction towards or preparation for it. (*S. th.* I–II, q. 106.) This interior energy of Christianity (*principalitas novæ legis*) does not exclude visible forms and institutions, but rather demands them. "Grace and truth have come to us through Jesus Christ. Therefore it is behooving that grace, on the one hand, flow upon us from the incarnate Word by means of sensible signs, and, on the other hand, that external sensible effects proceed from the internal grace through which the flesh is subordinated to the spirit. This gives us a double relation between external works and grace. Either our works lead to grace, as is the case with the sacraments of the New Law, Baptism, Eucharist, etc.; or external works are performed under the influence of grace" (*S. th.* I–II, q. 108, a. 1). Thomas embodies the sacramental factor in his notion of the Church. "Thus the sacraments form a main element in the Thomistic view of life; through them the ecclesiastical system acquires a mystical background and religious significance." [1]

---

[1] R. Eucken, *Die Lebensancshauungen der grossen Denker.* Leipzig, 1896, p. 157.

Co-ordinate with the sacraments is another element of his dogmatic conception of the Church, namely faith, the continuation of the truth of Christ in the Church. "Christianity, the law of the faith and of grace" (*Quodlib.* iv, 13).

These two basic elements, which signify the innermost life and being of the Christian religion, demand an external, divinely juridical ecclesiastical structure. If the Church is to be mediator of the grace and truth of Christ, and bring them to men, such an overflow of supernatural life must take place by means of certain organs united among themselves and with Christ. The idea of the Church necessarily demands for its realization a constitution and organization.

The dogmatic and divinely juridical aspects in Thomas' conception of Christianity and the Church show an ethico-mystical trend and character. The bond between Scholasticism and mysticism is seen in its fulness in the Thomistic teaching on the Church. This is evident from the picture which Thomas paints of the Christian, under the inspiration of Pauline writings: "He is called Christian who belongs entirely to Christ. A man belongs to Christ not only by belief in Christ, but by being imbued with the spirit of Christ unto works of virtue (Rom. 8, 9) and dying to his sins in the following of Christ" (*S. th.* II–II, q. 124, a. 5 ad 1).

[175]

Christianity is for Thomas the religion of love, freedom, perfection; an interior life is proper to the Christian. This aspect of interior life is a favorite point of emphasis. " The beauty of the Church consists chiefly in the inner life, in inner acts. External activities belong to this beauty in so far as they proceed from within and carefully preserve the inner beauty " (*In IV Sent.* d. 15, q. 3, a. 1, sol. 4). Love is the motive, the basic character of the Christian life; it is the bond that unites the members of the mystic body among themselves and with their common head Christ (*S. th.* II–II, q. 39, a. 1).

Closely related to this emphasis of the ethico-mystic element in the Church is Thomas' sympathetic understanding for mysticism and its importance in the life of the Church. The theological *summa* contains a profound study of mysticism (II–II, q. 179, ff.). In glowing words Thomas gives the preference to the contemplative life over the active (*l. c.*, 182, 1). From the ministers of the Church he demands a spirit of recollection and contemplation, and he increases his ethical demands according to the ranks of the hierarchy. For the higher ranks of the Church not only the virtues of active life are presupposed; " they must also shine in the contemplative life " (*S. th.* II–II, q. 182, a. 1 ad 1). " They must possess an eminent degree of divine love (*eminentia divinæ dilectionis*) " (*S. th.* II–II, q. 185, a. 3 ad 1).

In the inner spirit, in devotion to the things of God, Thomas also saw the deepest motive of celibacy (*S. th.* II–II, q. 152, a. 4–5).

All these elements are fused into an intimate unity in the Thomistic conception of the Church. In this harmony Thomas again shows himself a master of synthesis, the theologian of mediation and reconciliation. His theory skilfully avoids being one-sided. By emphasizing the inner values of Christianity, especially grace, the inner supernatural life, and loving fellowship with God, he does justice to the ideal, subjective element in the Church. By a proper estimate of the ecclesiastical organization, by emphasis on the objective character of the teaching office of the Church and the sacramental mediation of grace, he places the objective aspect in its correct light. Thus he occupies a middle position between an external and purely juridical conception of the Church, and a too subjective conception of the essence of the Church, one that would dissolve into a nebulous subjectivism.

Into this general picture of Christianity and the Church — they are the same for Thomas — his conception of the primacy fits harmoniously. In our own day it has again been said that Thomas was the first to introduce the idea of papal authority into Catholic dogmatic theology. Apart from the teaching of earlier theologians, this is false because before

Thomàs treated the question Bonaventure had already written a profound treatise " On the Obedience Due the Roman Pontiff," which is the most thorough exposition of this doctrine out of the golden period of Scholasticism. Some persons also claim that the spiritual and the hierarchical concepts of the Church are parallel or even opposed to each other in Thomas, and that his theory of the papacy was inspired by canon law and church politics. But against this stands the fact that Thomas derives his concept of the ecclesiastical power from the idea of Christ as the head of the Church (*S. th.* III, q. 8, a. 6). Especially is this view also contradicted by the manner in which Thomas establishes and develops the papal primacy in his *Summa contra gentes* (Bk. IV, ch. 76). Here he first shows that the highest ruling authority over the faithful belongs to the bishops. Then he adds his theological evidence for the primacy by establishing the fact that there must be one, namely the Pope, who is highest among the bishops. His proofs for this are as follows:

(a) *The concept of the Church as a Church of the whole world and of all nations.* Even if the Christian peoples are divided into various dioceses, there must ultimately be one Christian people, as also one Church. As there must be one bishop in each of the individual Christian nations, who is the head of a part of the people, so in the total union of

Christian people there must be one head of the entire Church.

(b) *The unity and purity of faith.* The unity of the faith demands that all the faithful agree in their creed. But many questions may arise concerning matters of faith. Diverse decisions in such questions would bring division into the Church. Only final decision by a single person can preserve unity. Hence follows the necessary demand for a single person at the head of the Church; and this essential demand of essence and unity of the Church has been realized. For it is clear that Christ did not deny to His Church anything that is necessary to it. He loved His Church and shed His blood for it. Hence there can be no doubt that Christ actually set up a single person as head of the Church.

(c) *Monarchy as the most perfect form of government.* There can be no doubt that the constitution of the Church is the most ideal and the best, since it comes from him by whom " kings reign, and lawgivers decree just things " (*Proverbs* 8, 15). The many are best governed by one, since the purpose of government is peace and unity. One individual can naturally attain unity better than many. Hence the constitution of the Church must be monarchical, and the Church must have a single head.

(d) *The relation of the Church Militant on earth to the Church Triumphant in heaven.* In the Church

Triumphant the ideal of monarchy is realized in the greatest degree, since all things are subject to God, Lord of the universe. Accordingly there must also be a single head over the Church Militant.

It were specious to say that this head, this single pastor, is Christ the one Bridegroom of the one Church. For the governing authority of the Church is in a position analagous to that of the sacramental means of grace. Christ Himself, indeed, produces all the sacramental effects in the Church. It is He who baptizes, forgives sins, is the true priest who offered Himself on the altar of the cross and in whose power the consecration of His body and blood takes place day by day on the altar. But as Christ no longer willed to remain here corporally and visibly, He chose servants to administer these sacraments to the faithful. In a similar way and for the same reason, He had to entrust His governing power over the entire Church to a representative. He actually gave this power to the apostle Peter, as we see from Matthew 16, 19, and John 21, 17. It lies in the purpose of this power that it continue in the successors of Peter after the latter's death. Christ instituted His Church so that it continue to exist till the end of the world.

Thus Thomas builds up the reality and necessity of the primacy speculatively out of the concept of the Church. He also has a high conception of the content and the extent of the papal power, as can be seen from a large number of passages. Still he is far from considering this power as unlimited. "There are things," he says (*In IV Sent.* d. 38, q. 1, a. 4), "in which man is so strictly his own master, that he can perform them even against the command of the Pope, as, e.g., continence and other divine counsels." The positive divine commands of revelation, and the natural moral law are irremovable boundaries for all authority. These ideas of Thomas on the Church and Church authority had an inspiring effect on subsequent times. Many of his immediate and later disciples wrote treatises on the ecclesiastical power. Thus we have in the thirteenth century and in the first years of the fourteenth the Augustinians Giles of Rome, Augustinus Triumphus, James of Viterbo, the Dominicans Hervæus Natalis, William Peter de Godin, Guido Vernani; in the fifteenth century, the Dominicans Henry Kalteysen, John Stojcovic of Ragusa, John of Montenegro, e.a. At the Council of Basil Torquemada compiled a monograph containing all the texts from Thomas bearing on the papal power; and he was the first to present a complete exposition of the subject in his big work "On the Church," in which there are many references to Thomas.

CHAPTER XIV

CONCLUSION. METHOD OF ACQUIRING A SCIENTIFIC
UNDERSTANDING OF THOMAS AQUINAS

HE leading position held by Thomas
for centuries in Catholic theology
and philosophy helps us to understand the increasing endeavor to
fathom the full meaning and interrelation of his writings, and the innumerable commentaries that resulted therefrom.
The *Summa contra gentes* has its classical commentator in Francis a Sylvestris of Ferrara. Armandus
de Bellovisu, Gerard de Monte, Versorius, Peter
Crockart, and Cardinal Cajetan expounded the *De
ente et essentia*. The *Quæstiones disputatæ* were in
part interpreted by Xantes Mariales. The commentaries on the *Summa theologica* are almost endless.
The era for this style of treatise set in towards the
end of the Middle Ages, when this maturest work of
Thomas gradually displaced the *Sentences* of Peter
the Lombard as the theological text of the higher
schools of learning. The series of commentaries was

commenced in German countries by Caspar Grun-
wald (Freiburg), Cornelius van Sneck (Rostock),
Hieronymus Dungersheim (Leipzig), and especially.
Conrad Koellin (Cologne); in Paris, by the Belgian
Peter Crockart; in Italy by Cardinal Cajetan; in
Spain by the disciple of Crockart, Franciscus de Vittoria, and his influential school. The greater number of the first commentators were Dominicans, soon
followed by theologians of the Society of Jesus, of
the Carmelites, etc., and by professors of the uni-
versities of Paris, Louvain, Douai, etc. In our own
day there has been a revival of commentaries on
Thomas. We have Latin commentaries on the
Summa theologica in whole or in part, by Satolli,
Billot, Lepicier, Del Prado, Buonpensiere, L. Jans-
sens, Paquet, Tabarelli, etc. An extensive commentary in French has been undertaken by Pègues.

This rich store of commentaries on the *summa* has
naturally also created a distinct method of interpret-
ing Thomas. We may call it the method of dialectical commentary. It proceeds by way of a logical
analysis of the text of Thomas, aiming at separating
the Thomistic doctrines into their conceptual elements. The main emphasis is directed towards indicating the order and inner coherence of the articles,
questions, treatises, and parts, and towards explaining
all the elements of the individual articles in as close
adherence to the words of Thomas as possible. For

this purpose a treatise is introduced by indicating its position in the respective part of the *summa* and its division into questions. At the beginning of every question the sequence of the articles is mentioned, and in the discussion of an article its title is first explained and thus the point at issue stated. Then in the body of the article the solution of the question begins with a general outline of the philosophical and theological principles and concepts that Thomas used in his answer, whereupon the content and argumentation of his solution is presented in clearly defined conclusions, generally in syllogistic form. The objections mentioned and refuted by Thomas are generally given *in forma,* that is, in syllogisms. Often too, especially when the passage is less clear, parallel texts from other writings of Thomas are cited according to the principle formulated by A. Massoulié: Thomas is his own best interpreter. There are undoubtedly great advantages in this exegetical method, which was specially fostered by the general chapters and the constitutions of the Dominicans, and became traditional among the theologians of the order. It leads to great familiarity with the texts of Thomas, to a deep insight into the coherence of his teachings, shows the rigorous consistency of his system, and gives a good picture of the structure and architectonic of his theological *summa.*

But this method of dialectical commentary gives us only one view of the teachings of Thomas. It analyzes and dissects the latter as a completely given whole.

It is a just demand of the modern scientific mind that the genesis of a theory out of previous elements be investigated. Such an historical method sheds light on the position of a theory in the general development of the science, and tries to understand a great mind from its relation to its own time and environment. The method is all the more appropriate with regard to an author who has not spun his system *a priori* out of his inner consciousness, but has rather like Thomas absorbed all the elements of previous learning and synthesized them into a unified system of thought. The dialectical method must, therefore, be supplemented and corrected by the historico-genetic method. The task of the latter would be to analyze the thought of Thomas into its historical components, and to indicate its development out of the philosophy and theology of previous and contemporary thinkers, and at the same time to point out the sources indicating the influence of Thomistic thought on contemporary and subsequent minds.

Various means are applicable in the solution of this task. Above all there is the study of sources, which must answer the question: What materials did Thomas have at his disposal and what use did he make of them? In this study his relation to the Scriptures and the Fathers, especially to Augustine, to Aristotle and the Arabian-Jewish philosophy, the Neoplatonic theories, to the thinkers of early Scholasticism, to his immediate predecessors, and to his contemporaries, must be investigated. The study of unpublished *sentences* or *summæ* in particular, like those of Robert of Melun, Martin of Cremona, Simon of Tournai, Præpositinus, Philip of Greve, Roland of Cremona, etc., will shed much light on the antecedents of many a Thomistic viewpoint. There are still many obscure points on the relation of Thomas to the printed works of William of Auxerre, Alexander of Hales, Albert the Great, etc. And the use Thomas made of Aristotle can be appraised completely only after clear knowledge has been attained on the different aspects of the acceptance and the translations of Aristotle. Again the entire teaching of Thomas will come out in bolder relief by comparative study with the views of contemporary thinkers. Good service for the historical understanding of Thomas will also be rendered by a more detailed knowledge of the external conditions that were influential in the scientific life and endeavor of the time. Such factors would be, for instance, the development of higher studies and teaching in Paris, the theological questions and disputes that occupied the minds of the day, the history of the Dominican and Franciscan orders, etc. In this way it will be possible to delineate the historical background in which Thomas appears, and especially to reconstruct, in part at least, a bibliography of the works on which he drew.

Another aim of the historical investigation should be to outline the development of Thomas himself. Thomas improved and clarified his thought in many points, perfected earlier ideas in later works, corrected them, or even retracted them when necessary. There are several noteworthy indications of this in his own statements, as also in some compilations by his pupils preserved to us in manuscript form. In order better to establish and adjudge such a development in him, it will be necessary to keep in mind the chronology of his writings. Naturally the certainly genuine works of Thomas will have to be separated from the dubious or even spurious ones.

Another task for the historical study of Thomas will be to establish the opinions his contemporaries had of his various views, and especially to learn the views of his immediate and mediate disciples. It is evident that the polemical literature that arose between the scientific opponents and the faithful disciples of Thomas after his death will shed much light on his exact teaching. In this controversial literature, of which some mention was made above, just those points of his teaching are brought out which are characteristic of him and represent new and independent work on his part. In defence of their master the disciples of Thomas had to clear up all possible misunderstandings of his thought, and to present the most definite picture possible of his views. There can be no doubt that their personal contact with him makes them more reliable interpreters of the meaning and spirit of his teachings than the commentators living some centuries later, who were dependent entirely on the dead letter of the text. We should, therefore, be able to get much light from the immediate and mediate disciples of Thomas on some points that are controverted because of the brevity and difficulty of his text.

Such are in short the chief roads on which the historico-genetic method must proceed in order to find out the manner and circumstances of the origin, the development, and the later influence of his writings. It is not necessary to mention that for such work familiarity with modern philological-historical method, especially knowledge of palæography, is indispensable. The historical study of Thomas had its champions also in earlier times. The Dominicans Antonius Senensis, Nocolai, Quétif, Echard, de Rubeis, and others, deserve much credit for their studies on textual criticism and questions of authenticity. Many works of former days show that the need of a comparative study of Thomas and other Scholastics was also felt; e.g., the great works of Macedo, Rada, and others, on Thomas and Scotus; of Bonherba a S. Philippo on Thomas, Scotus, and Giles of Rome; of Lardico and Saenz d'Aguirre on Thomas and Anselm; of Bonaventura Lingonensis, Marcus de Baudunio, and others, on Thomas and Bonaventure. In more recent times, we cannot omit the outstanding merit of the Italian priest Pietro Uccelli (d. 1880) in the examination of Thomistic manuscripts. Denifle long considered the plan of writing a commentary on the *Summa theologica* from the historical standpoint and from that of a critical study of source materials. Even if he did not realize this plan, his occasional contributions added considerably to a better understanding of the speculative thought of Thomas. Much of the present ever-increasing study and research in this field dates back to the inspiration of Denifle.

The historico-genetic method of studying Thomas, the purpose, means, and ways of which we have mentioned, possesses real advantages. It is a welcome complement to the method of dialectical commentary, and a reliable guide to a more profound and universal understanding, and to a correct appraisal, of the teachings of Thomas.

We have already stated that a knowledge of the manner in which his thought affected his contemporaries and especially his followers, will be a great help in defining the more obscure and controverted points of his writings. Such a study leads us into the intellectual workshop of Aquinas, into the ideals and the means of his scientific study, and gives us, as it were, a new and living picture of the life-work of the great thinker. In the light of an investigation of sources and of a comparative study, we can best see his development in method and content, and the degree of his dependence as of his originality. We thus get to see Thomas as a theologian who was modern in his own time, who made use of the results of past and present, and in many questions saw far beyond his contemporaries. The historical method also permits us to draw a clearer line between that which was of importance rather for his own time, conditioned by the circumstances and questions of his own day, and that which is of more lasting value. It will also reveal to us the immensity of his genius for systematization. Just as in an artistic fabric we see the great skill of the work only after examining in detail the innumerable variety of interwoven threads, so we also see the genial architectonic powers of Aquinas completely only when an analysis of sources has shown us the different elements and materials that his harmonizing and synthetic mind formed into a great whole. A final advantage of the historical method is a negative one, in so far as it guards us from the danger of falsely projecting the ideas, questions, and phraseology of later schools back into the medieval Scholasticism and especially into the speculation of Thomas.

In this way the methods of dialectic commentary and of historic origins supplement each other and give us a broad, scientific conception of the ideas of the greatest philosopher and theologian of the Middle Ages.